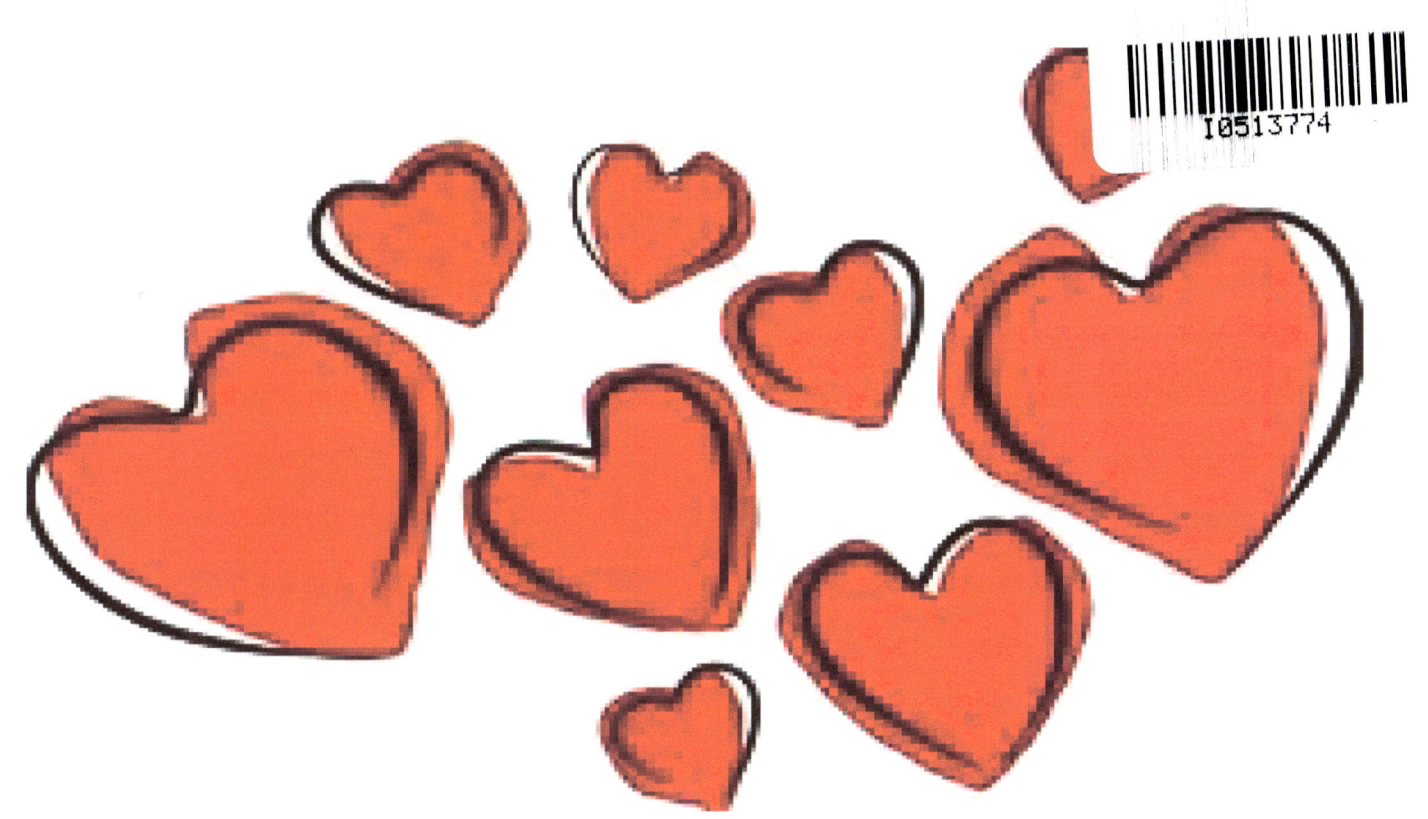

The classic story of Romeo and Juliet, set in a modern-day city of Verona Beach.

The Montagues and Capulets are two feuding families, whose children meet and fall in love.

They have to hide their love from the world because they know that their parents will not allow them to be together.

"My bounty is as boundless as the sea, Mty love as deep; the more I give to thee, The more I have, for both are intimate"

SPOKEN BY JULIET

ROMEO AND JULIET, ACT 2, SCENE 2

Romeo and Juliet quotes are some of Shakespeare's most popular, and the play is full of enduring quotes from start to grisly finish.

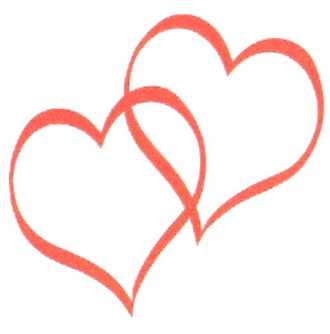

"A pair of star-crossed lovers take their life."

(Chorus, Prologue)

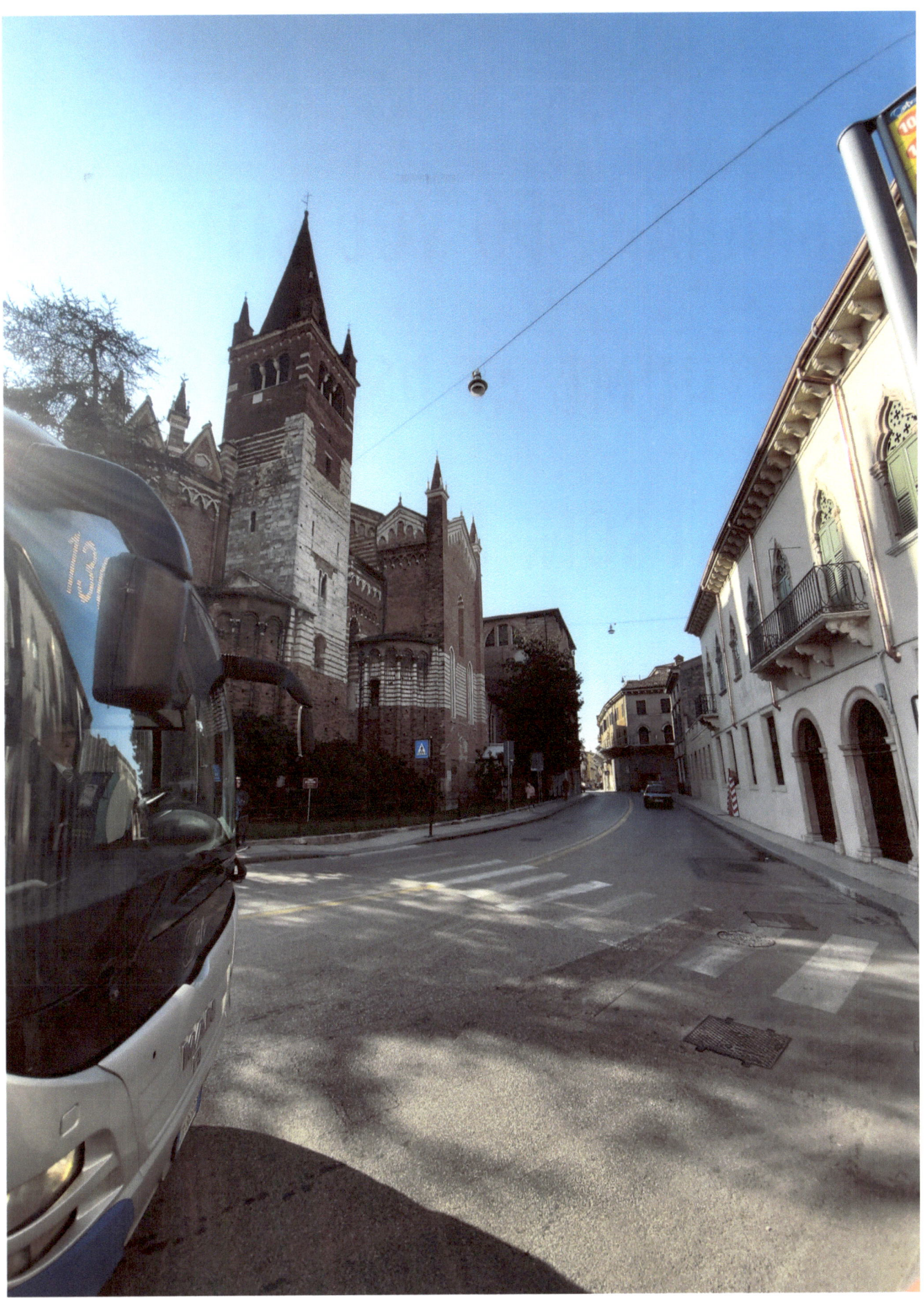

"Abraham: Do you bite your thumb at us, sir?
Sampson: I do bite my thumb, sir."
(Act 1, Scene 1)

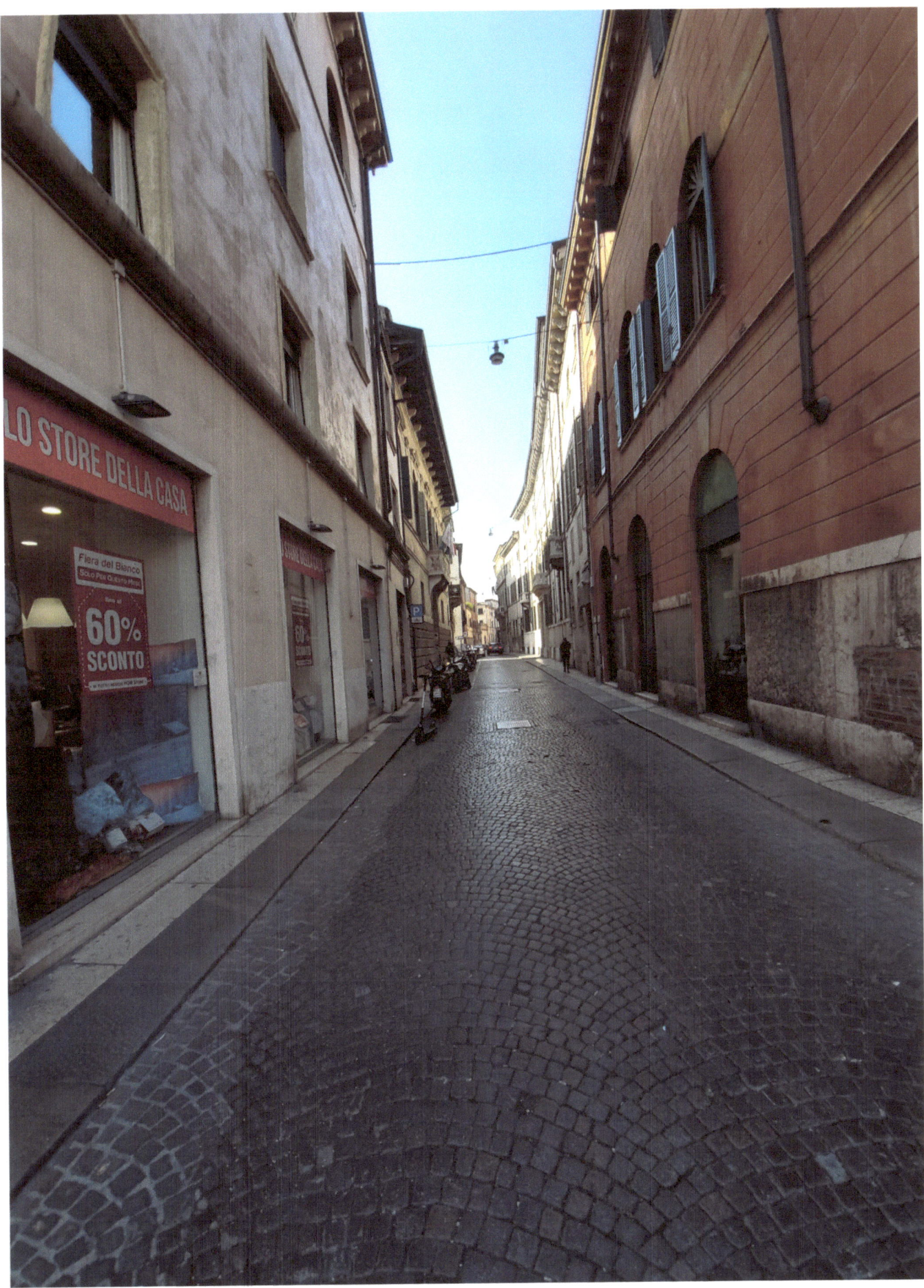

"O teach me how I should forget to think!"
Romeo (act 1 scene 1)

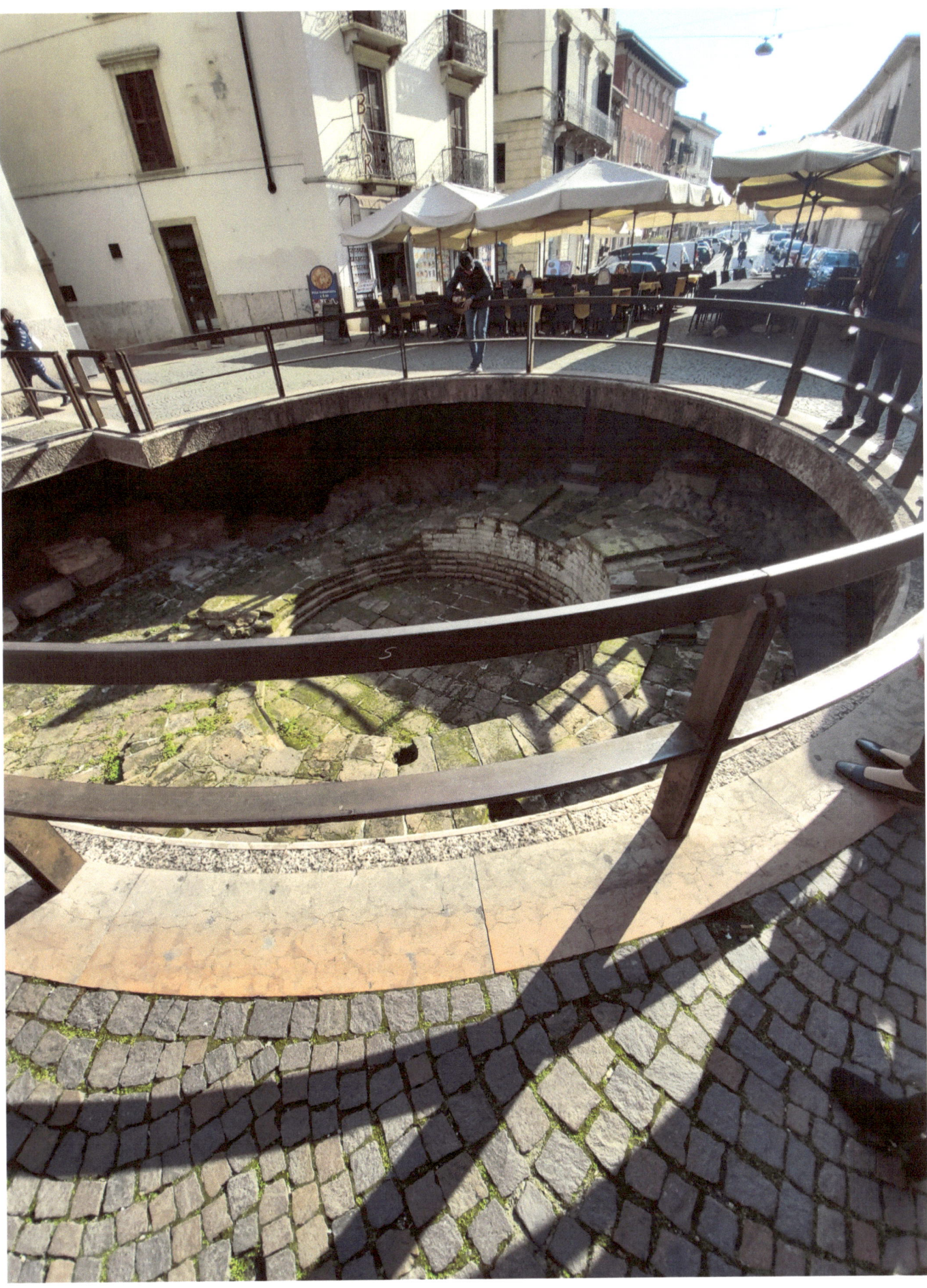

Love is a smoke made with the fume of sighs.
Being purged, a fire sparkling in lovers' eyes;
Being vex'd a sea nourish'd with lovers' tears."
Romeo ( act 1 scene 1)

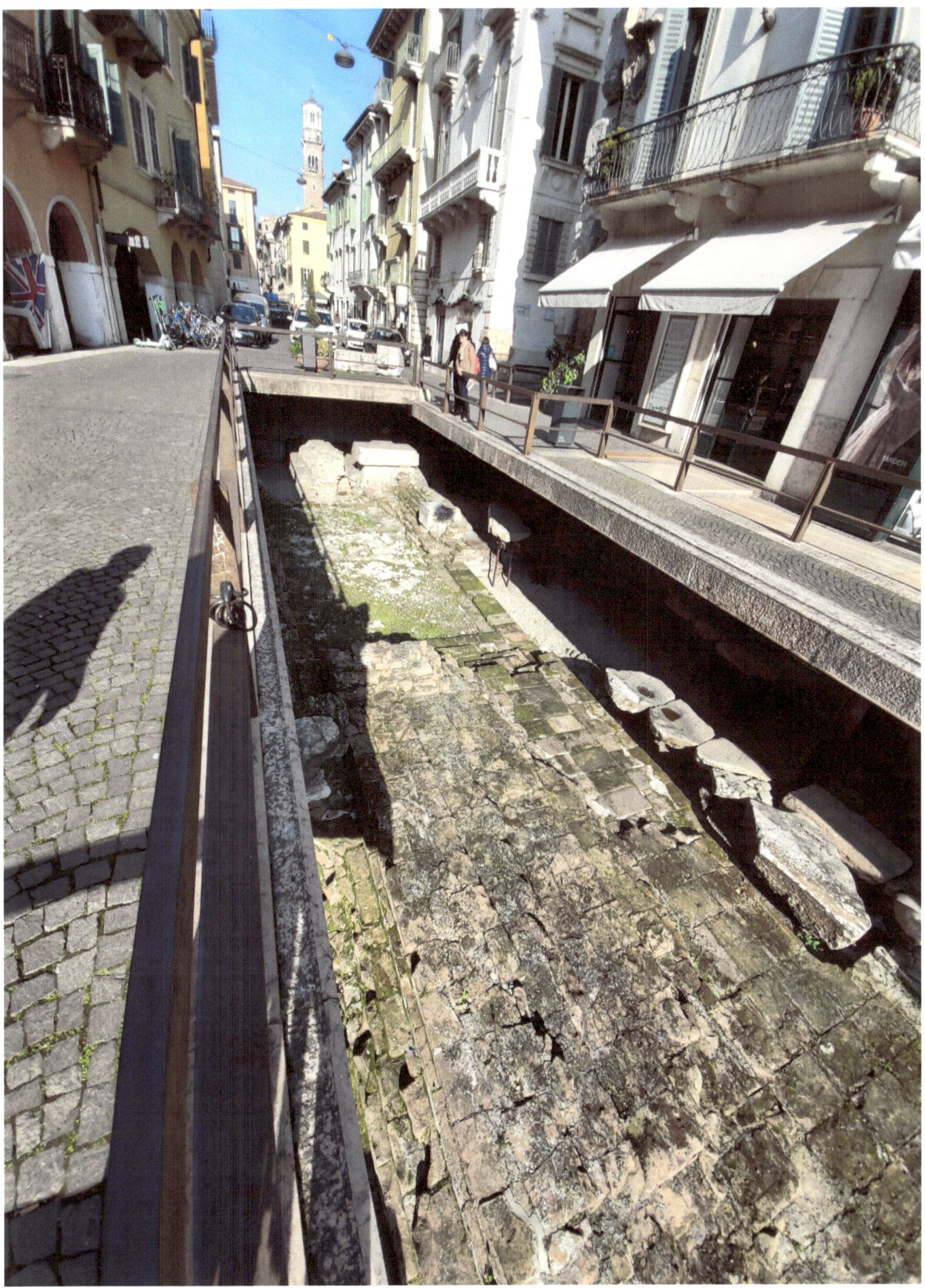

"Under loves heavy burden do I sink."

Romeo (act 1 scene 4)

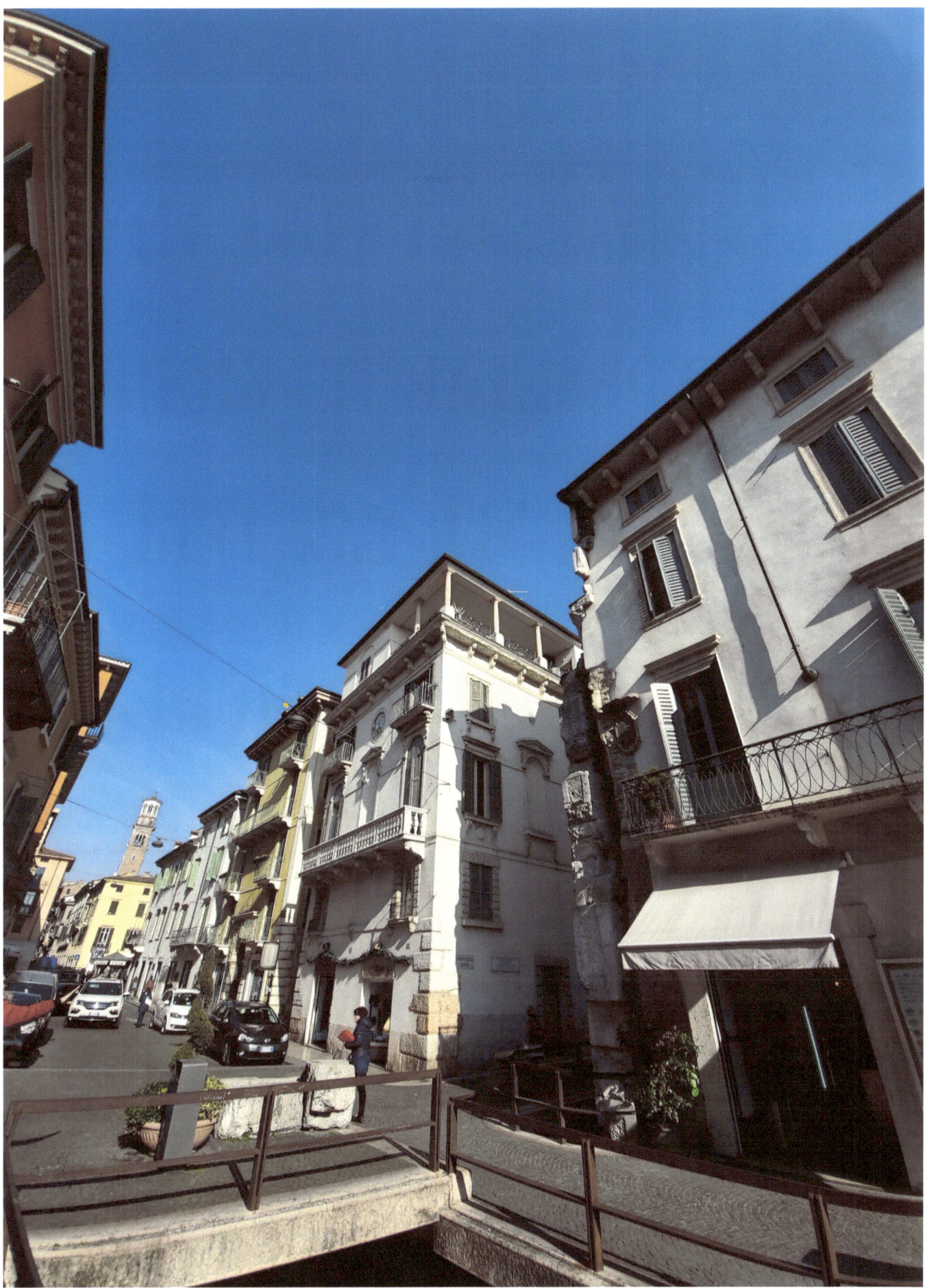

"Did my heart love till now? Forswear it, sight! For I ne'er saw true beauty till this night."
Romeo (act 1 scene 5)

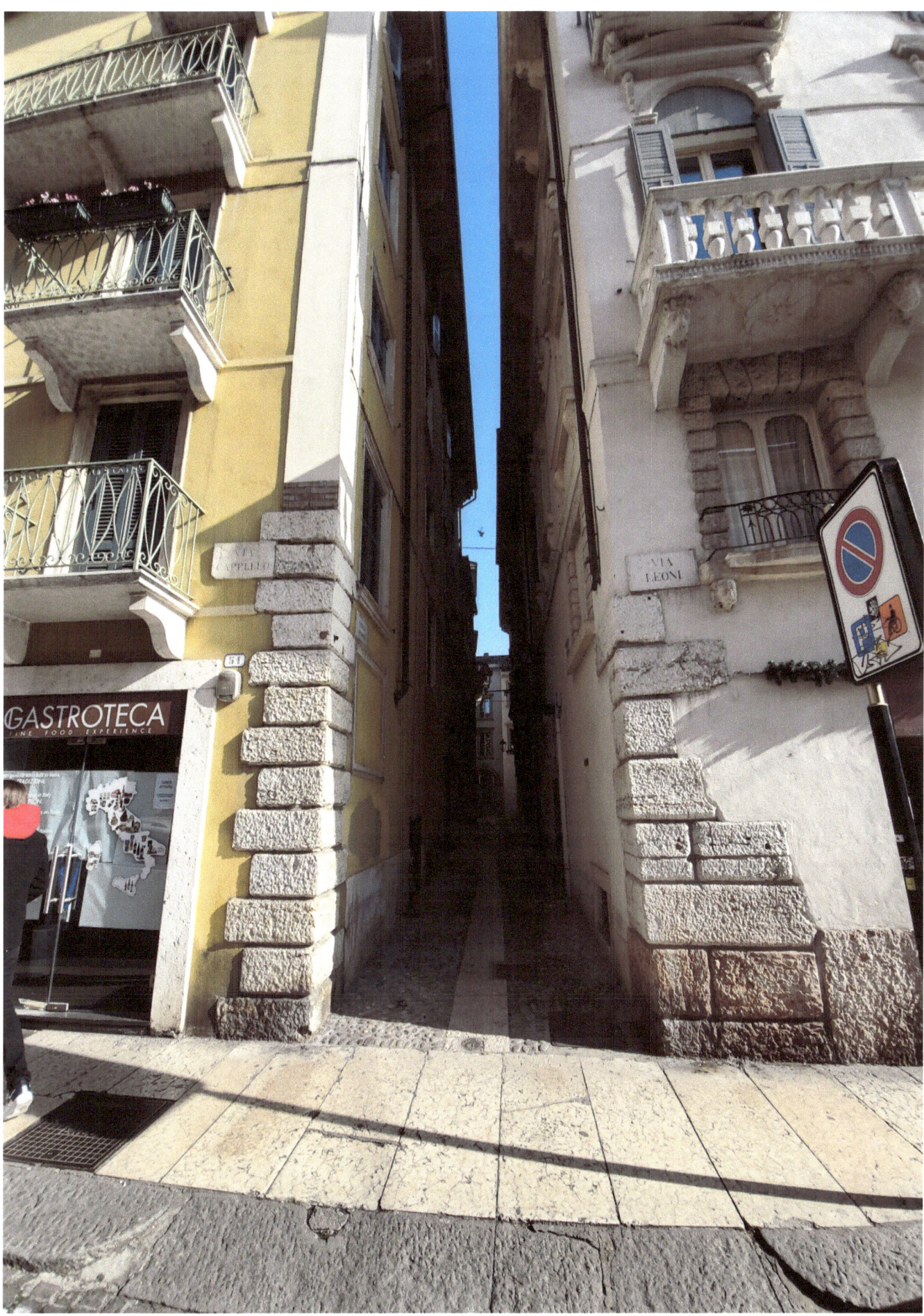

"O, she doth teach the torches to burn bright."
Romeo (act 1 scene 5)

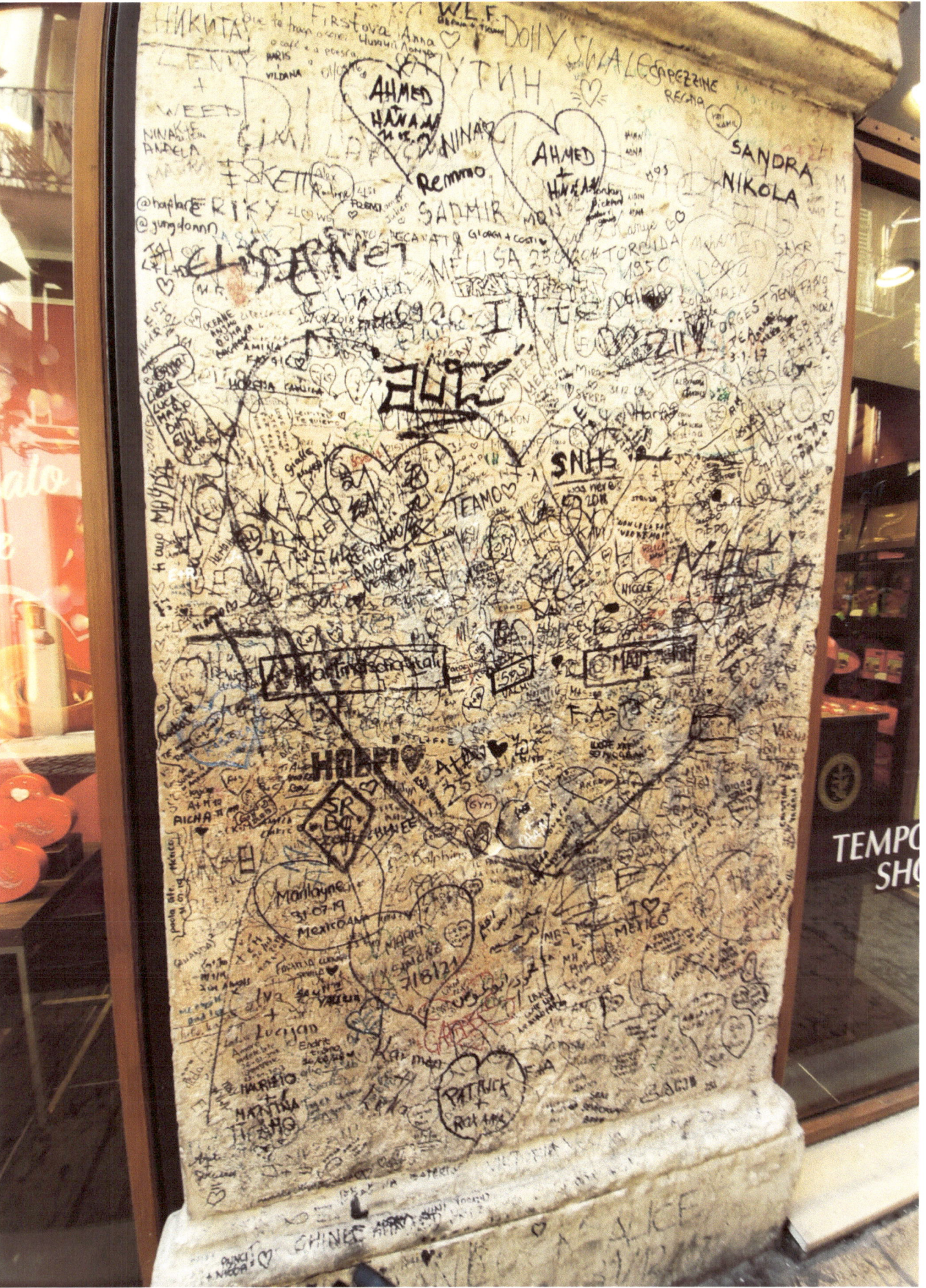

"But, soft, what light through yonder window breaks?
It is the east, and Juliet is the sun."
Romeo (act 2, scene 2)

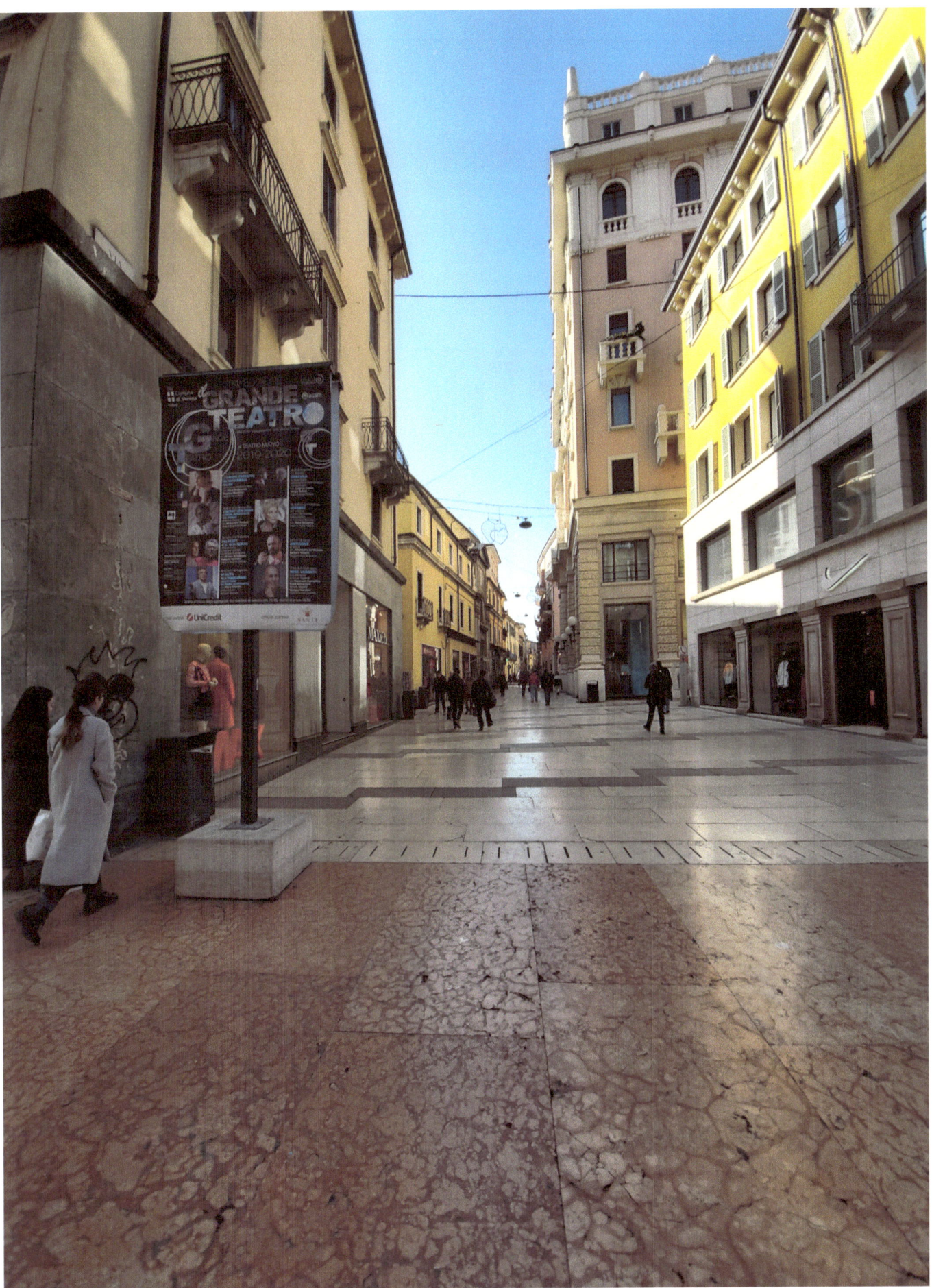

"O Romeo, Romeo, wherefore art thou Romeo?"

Juliet ( act 2 scene 2)

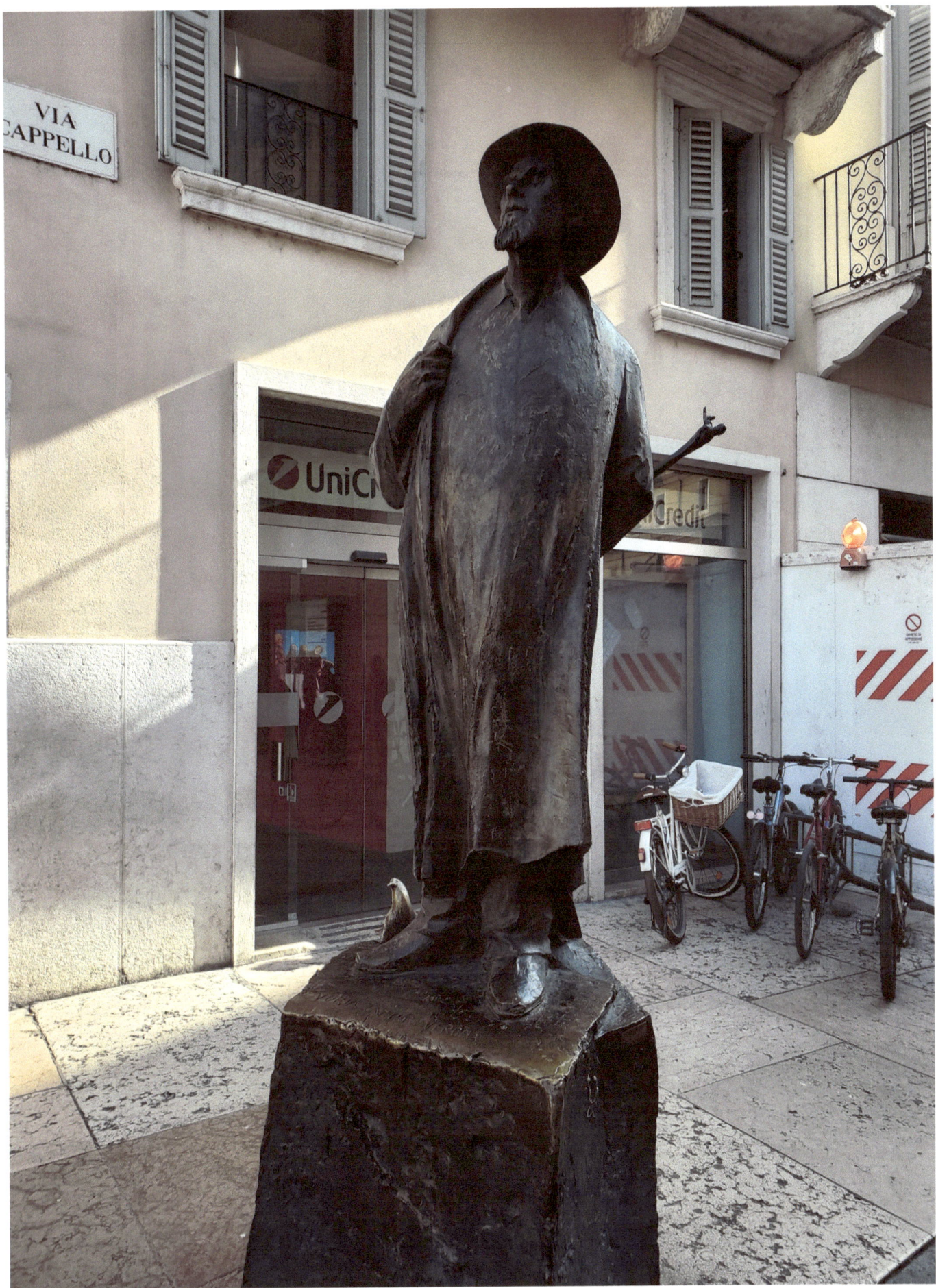

"That which we call a rose
By any other name would
smell as sweet."
Juliet (act 2, scene 2)

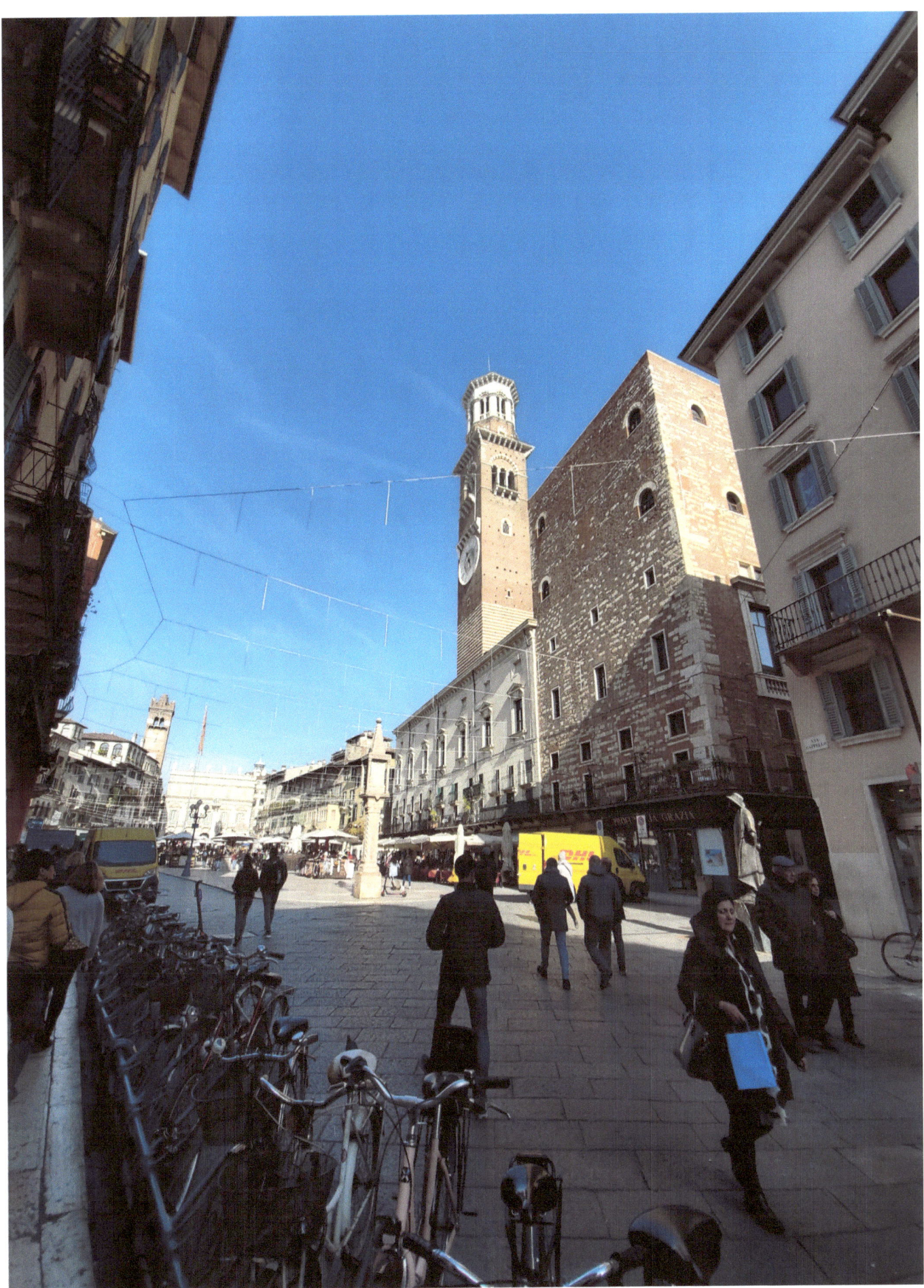

"See how she leans her cheek upon her hand. O, that I were a glove upon that hand That I might touch that cheek!"

Romeo (Act 2, Scene 2)

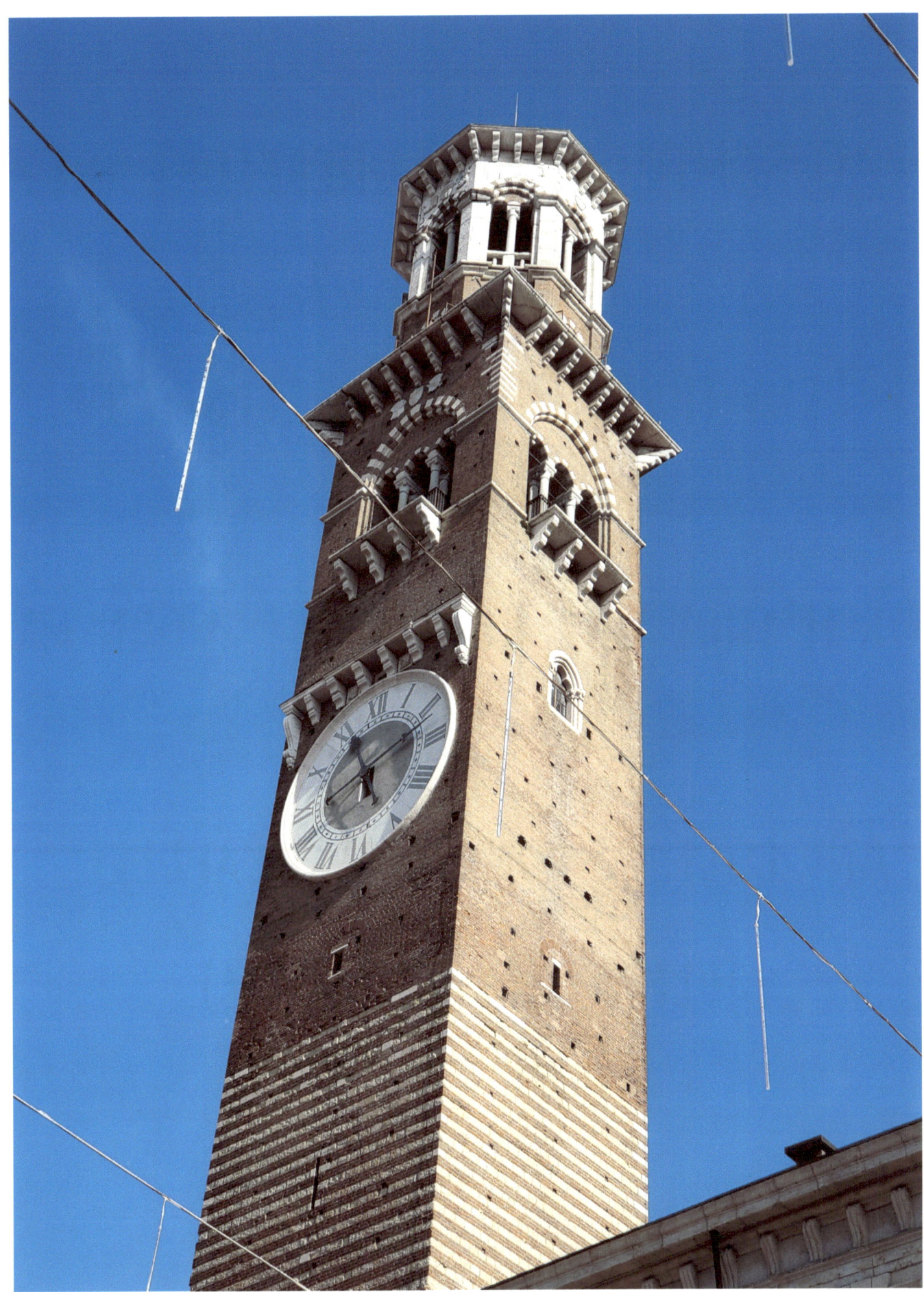

"O Romeo, Romeo, wherefore art thou Romeo?
Deny thy father and refuse thy name;
Or if thou wilt not, be but sworn my love
And I'll no longer be a Capulet."
Juliet (act 2, scene 2)

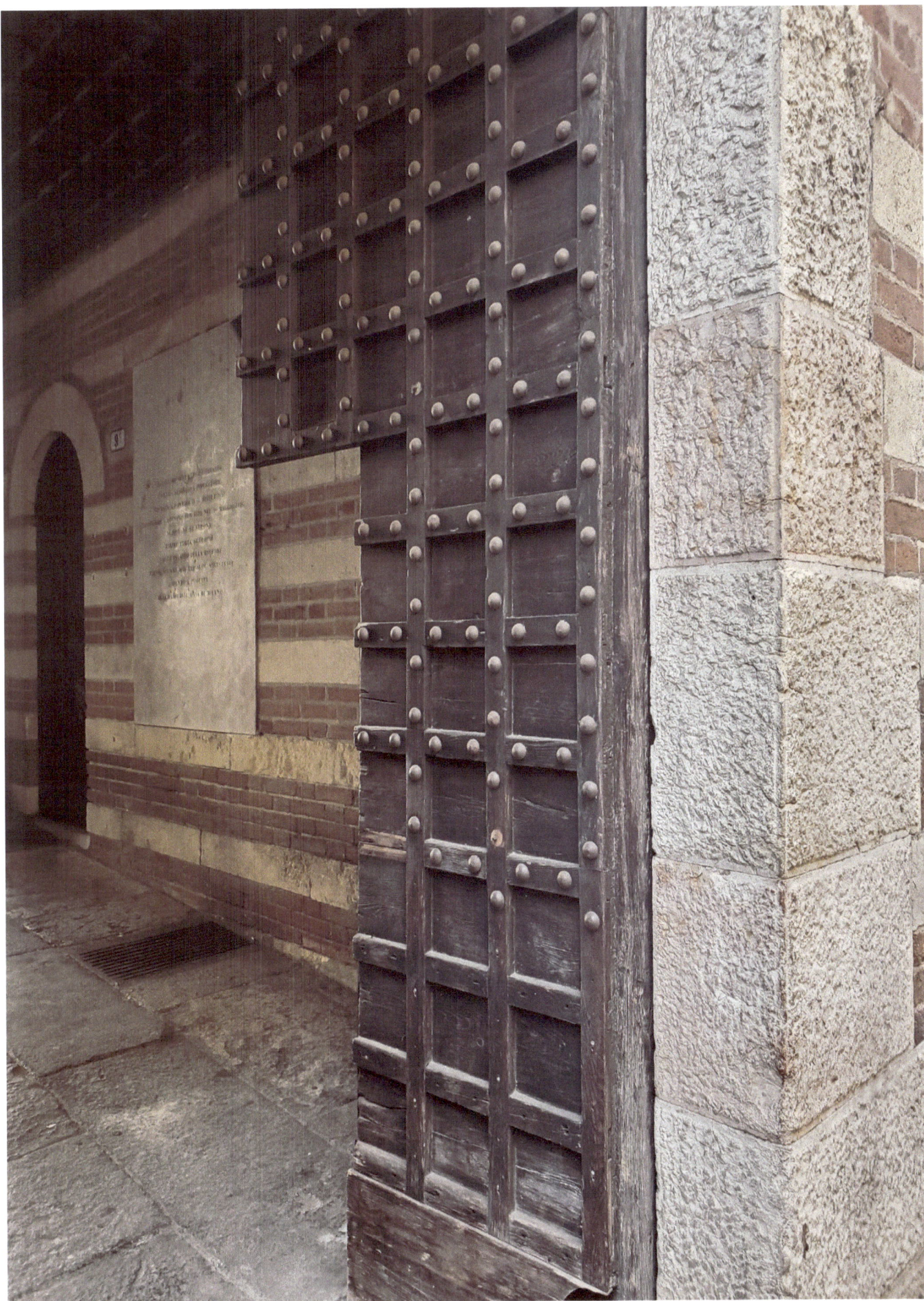

"O, swear not by the moon, th' inconstant moon, That monthly changes in her circle orb, Lest that thy love prove likewise variable."
Juliet (Act 2, Scene 2)

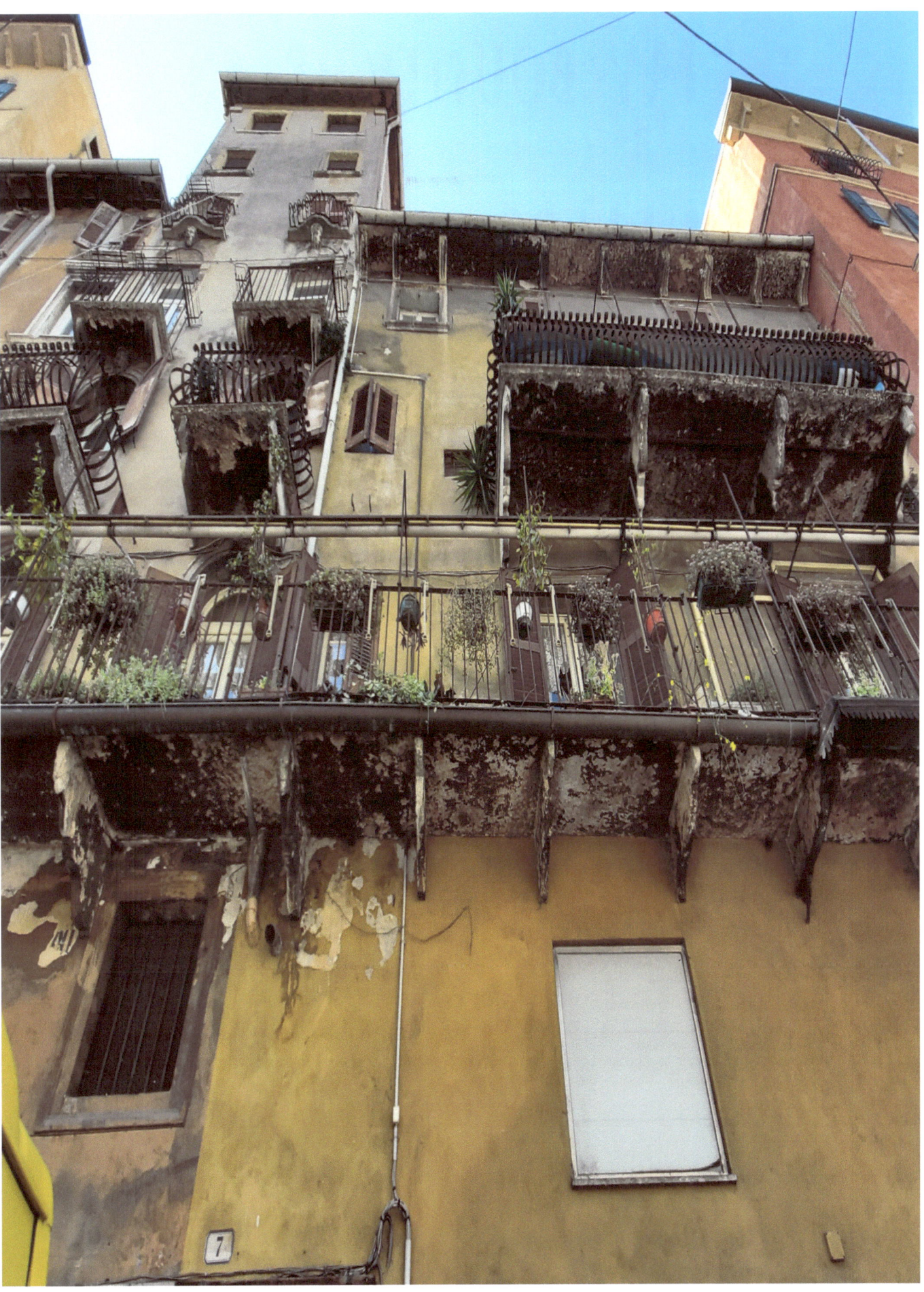

"My bounty is as boundless as the sea, My love as deep; the more I give to thee, The more I have, for both are infinite."

Juliet (Act 2, Scene 2)

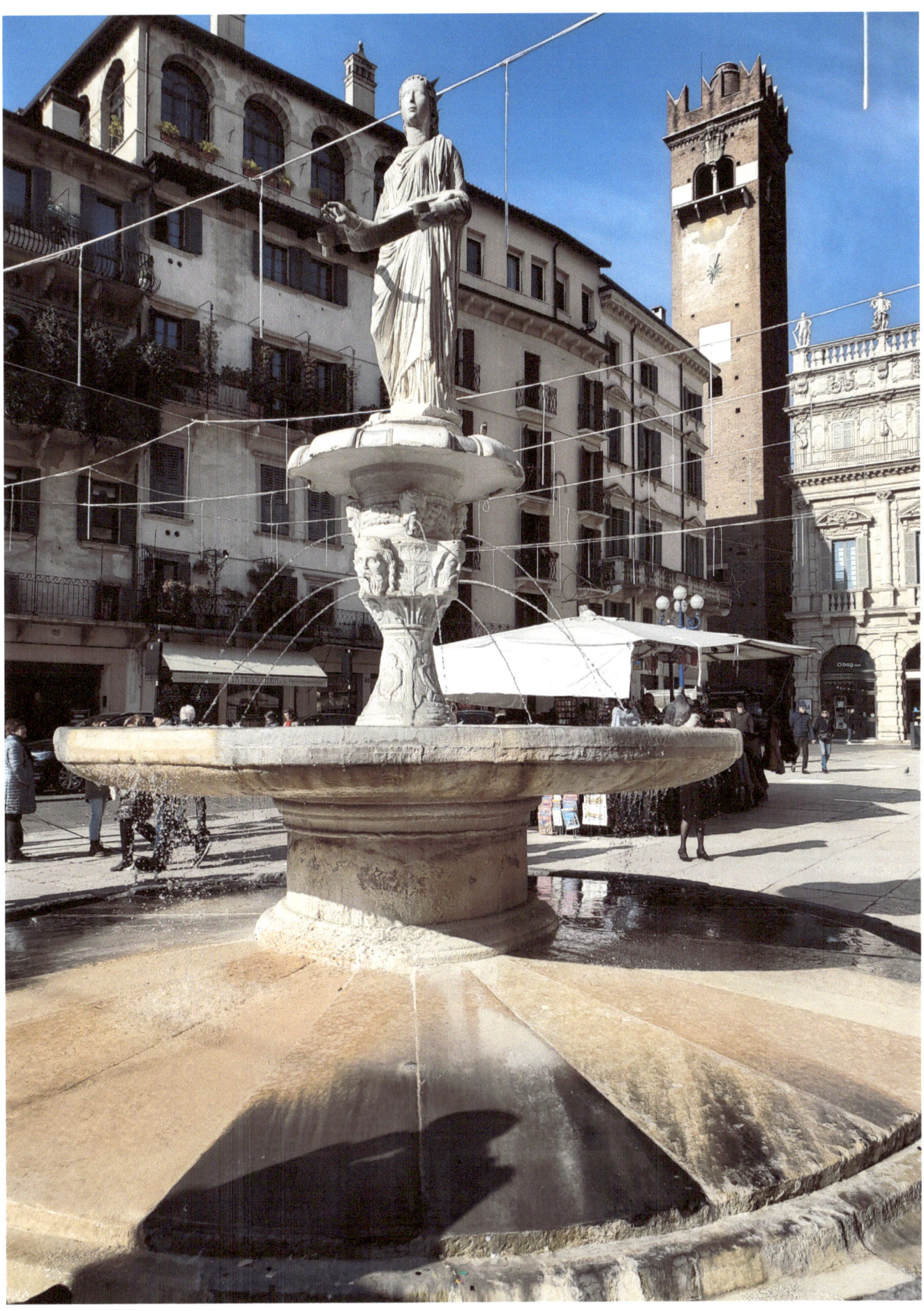

"This bud of love, by summer's ripening breath, may prove a beauteous flower when next we meet."

Juliet (act 2, scene 2)

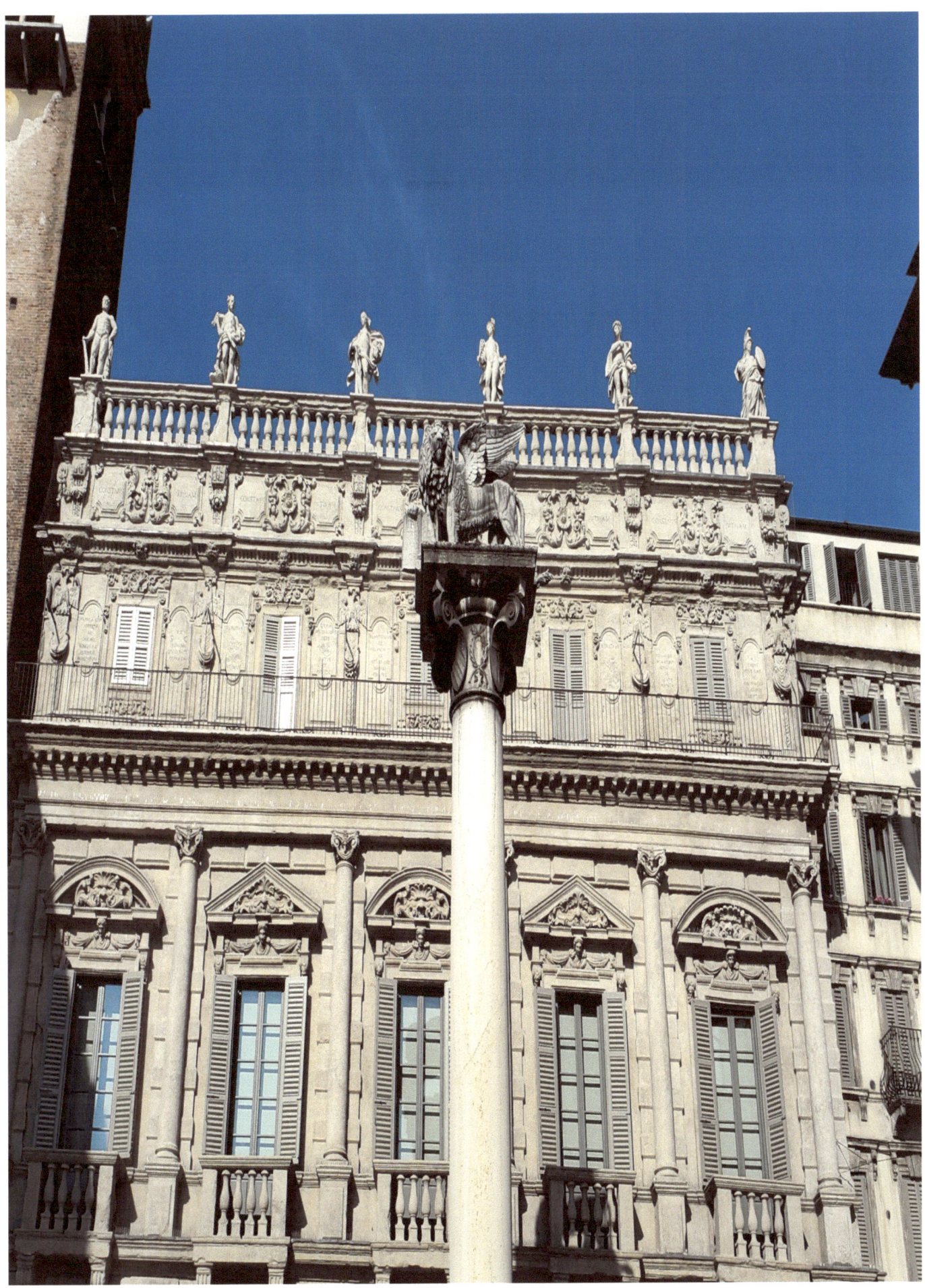

Good night, good night! Parting is such sweet sorrow,
That I shall say good night till it be morrow

Juliet (act 2, scene 2)

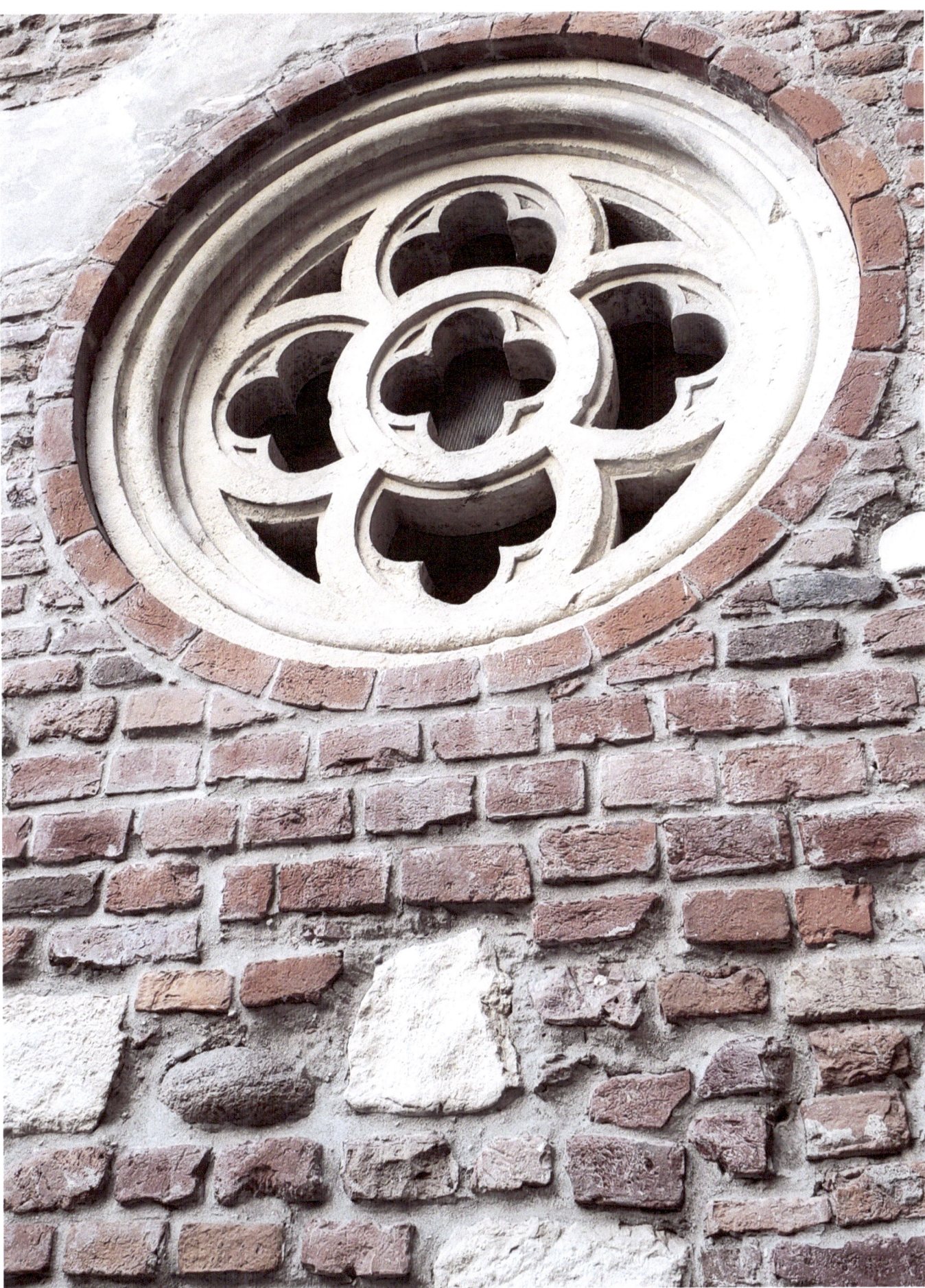

"Wisely and slow; they stumble that run fast."
Friar Laurence (act 2, scene 3)

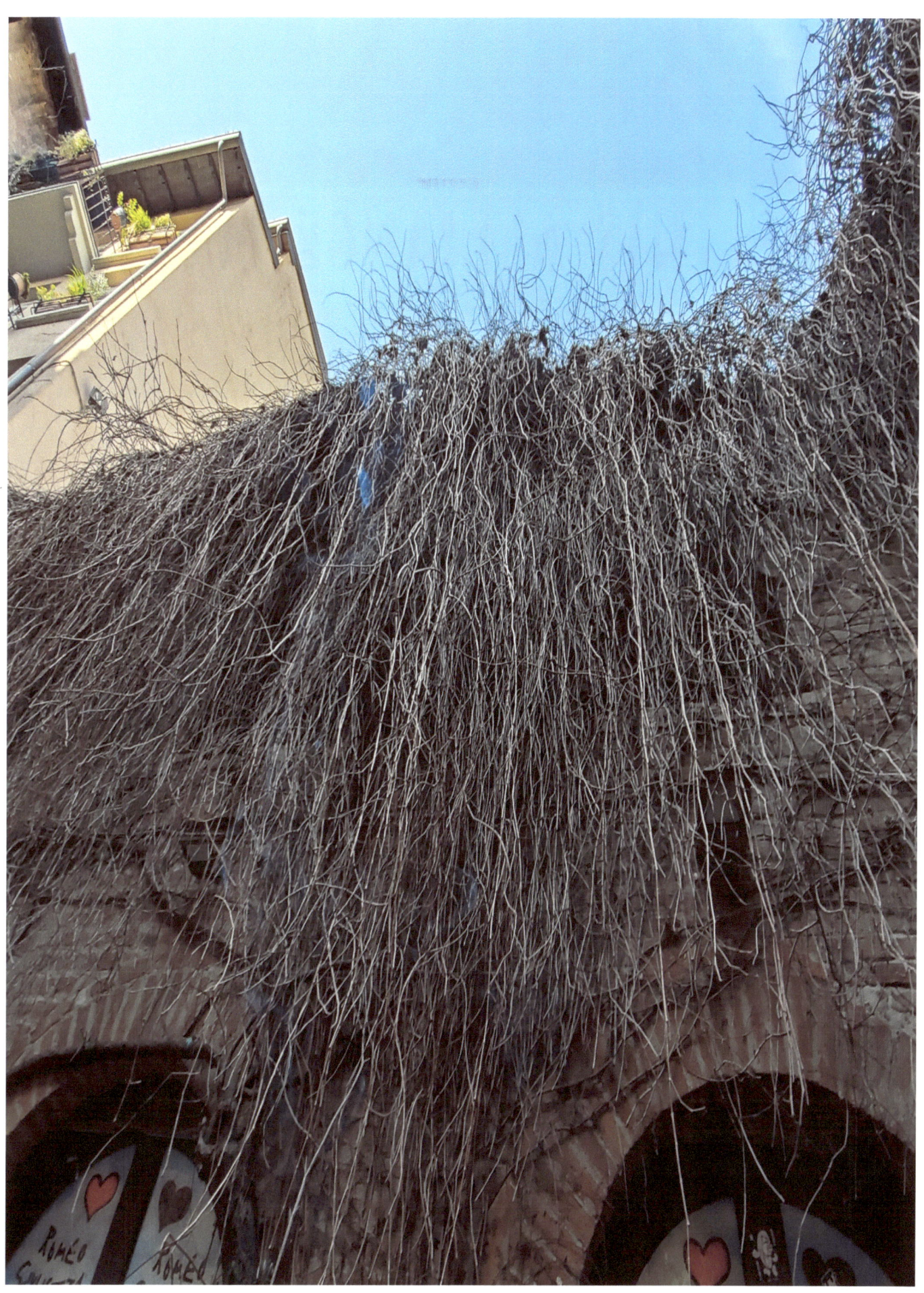

"For this alliance may so happy prove,
To turn your households' rancour to pure love."
Friar Laurence (act 2, scene 3)

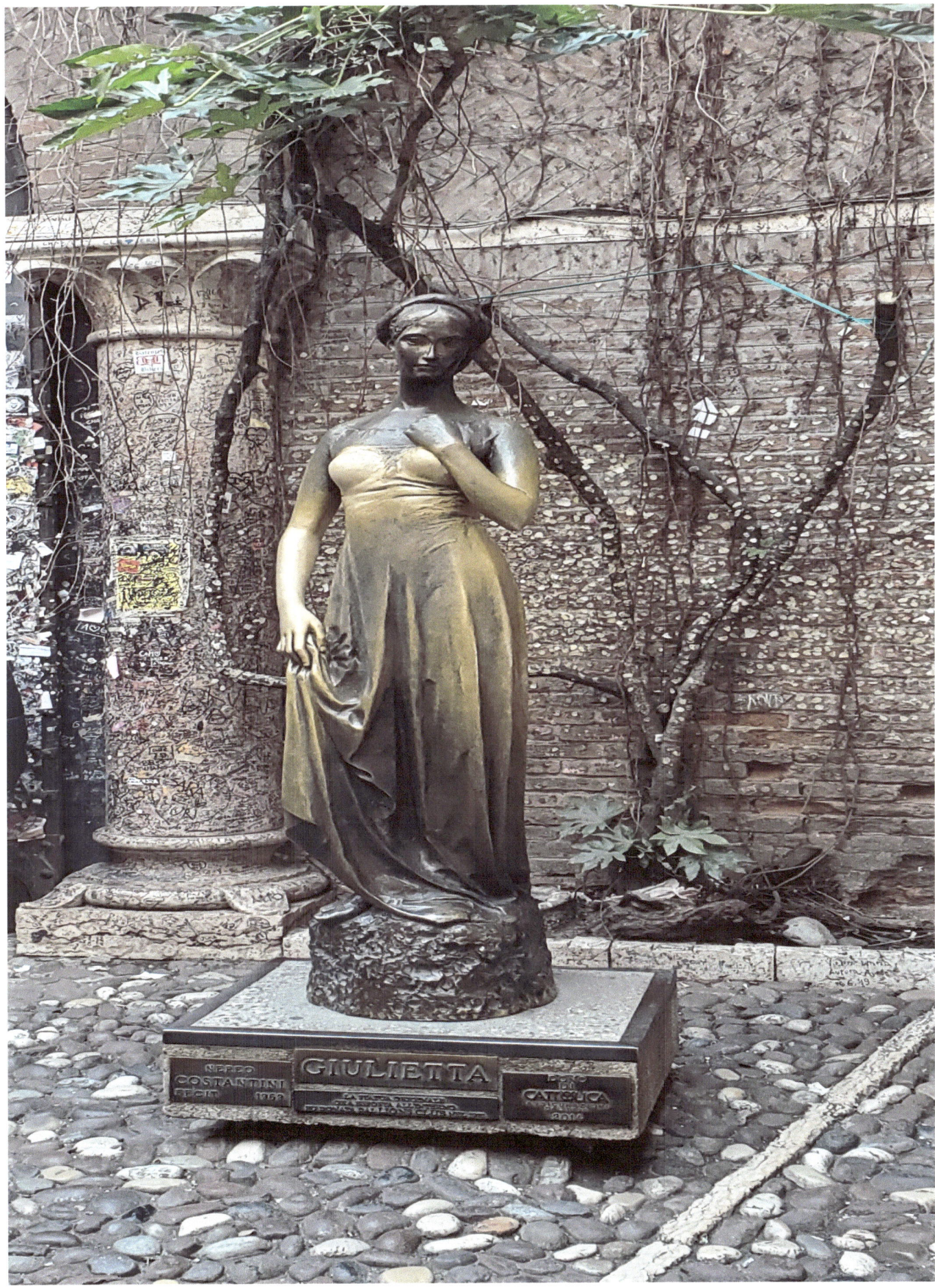

"Women may fall when there's no strength in men."
Friar Laurence (Act 2, Scene 3)

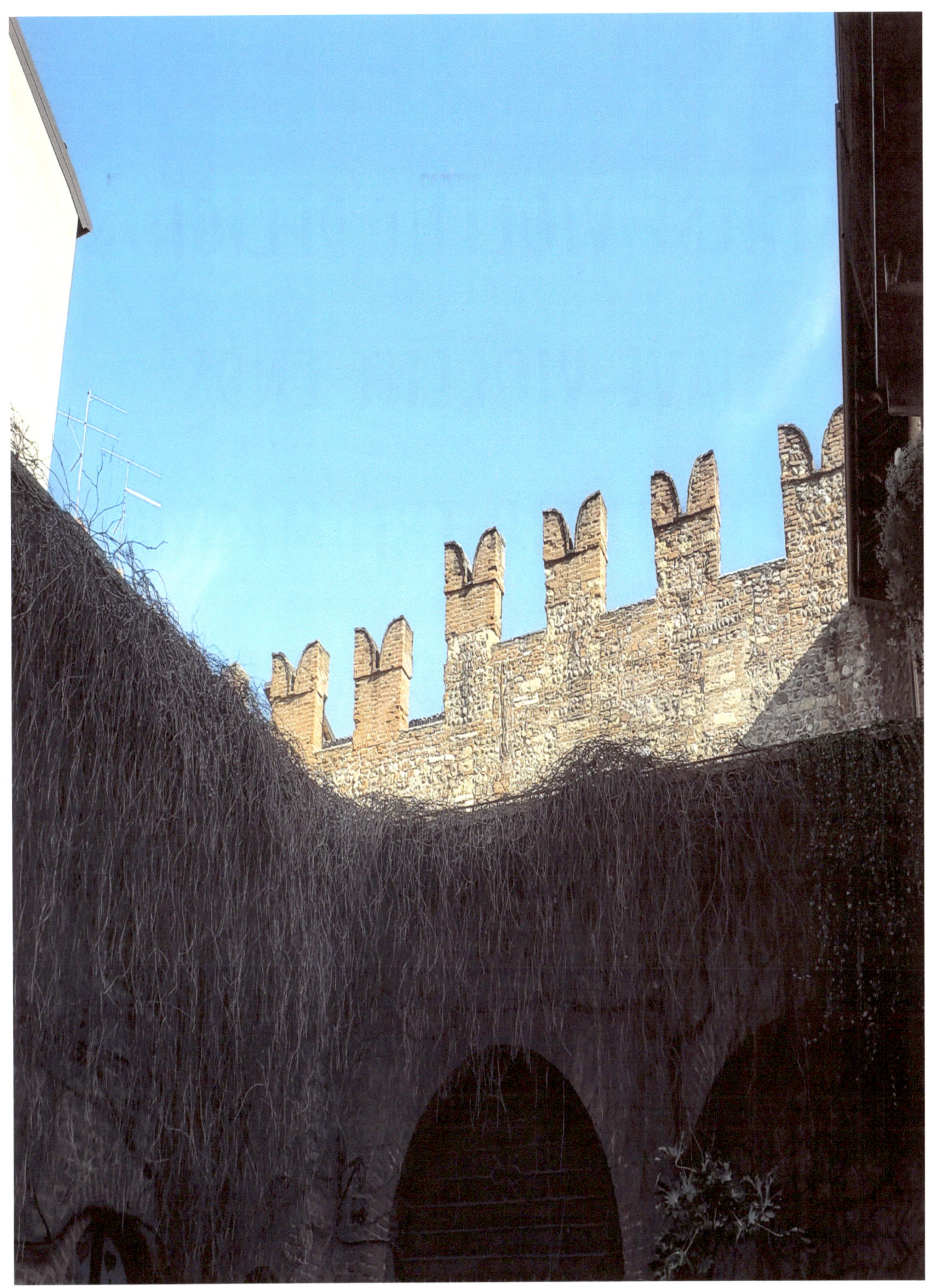

"These violent delights have violent ends And in their triumph die, like fire and powder" Friar Laurence (act 2, scene 5)

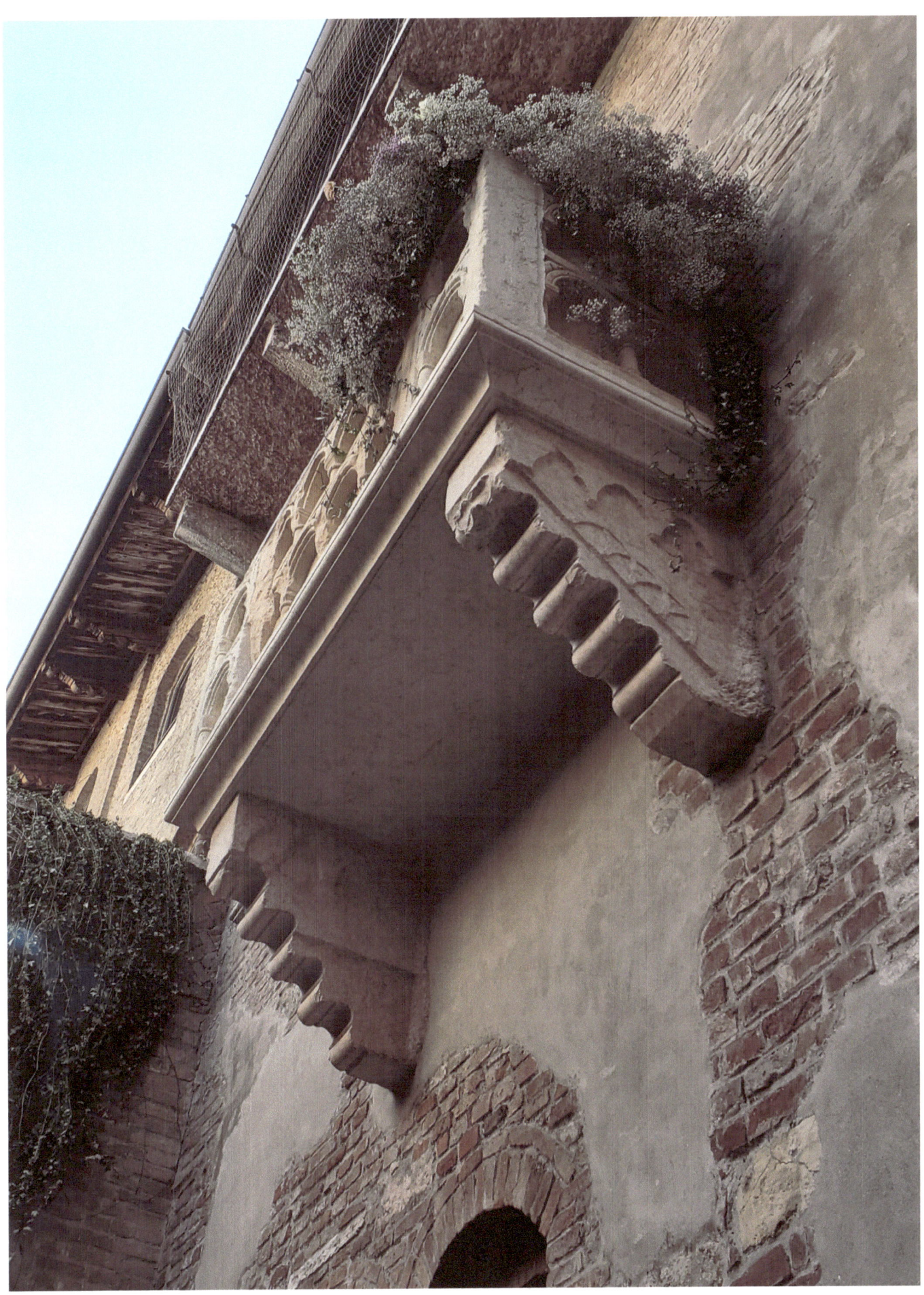

"A plague o' both your houses!"

Mercutio (act 3, scene 1)

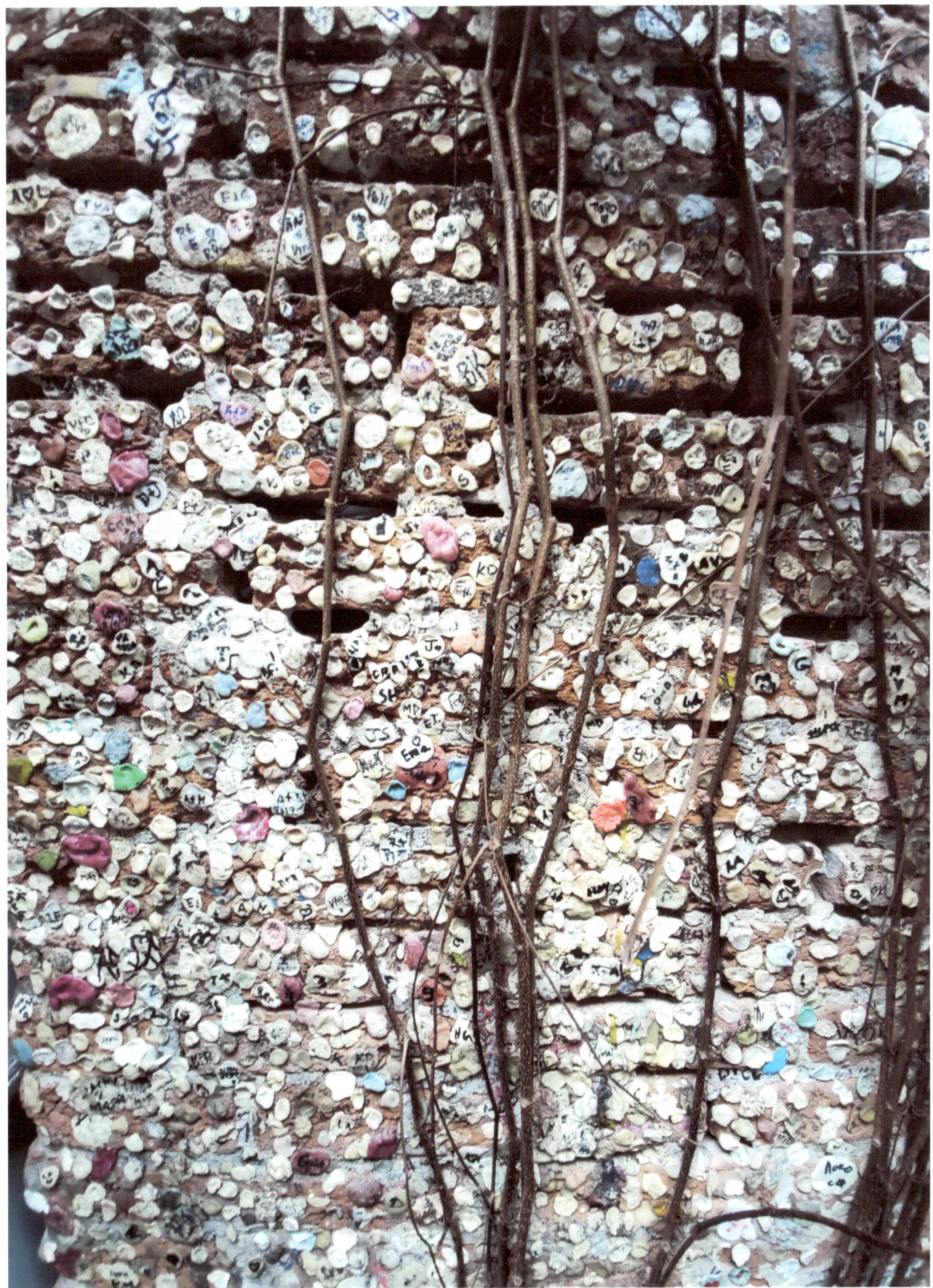

"Mercy but murders, pardoning those that kill."
Prince (act 3, scene 1)

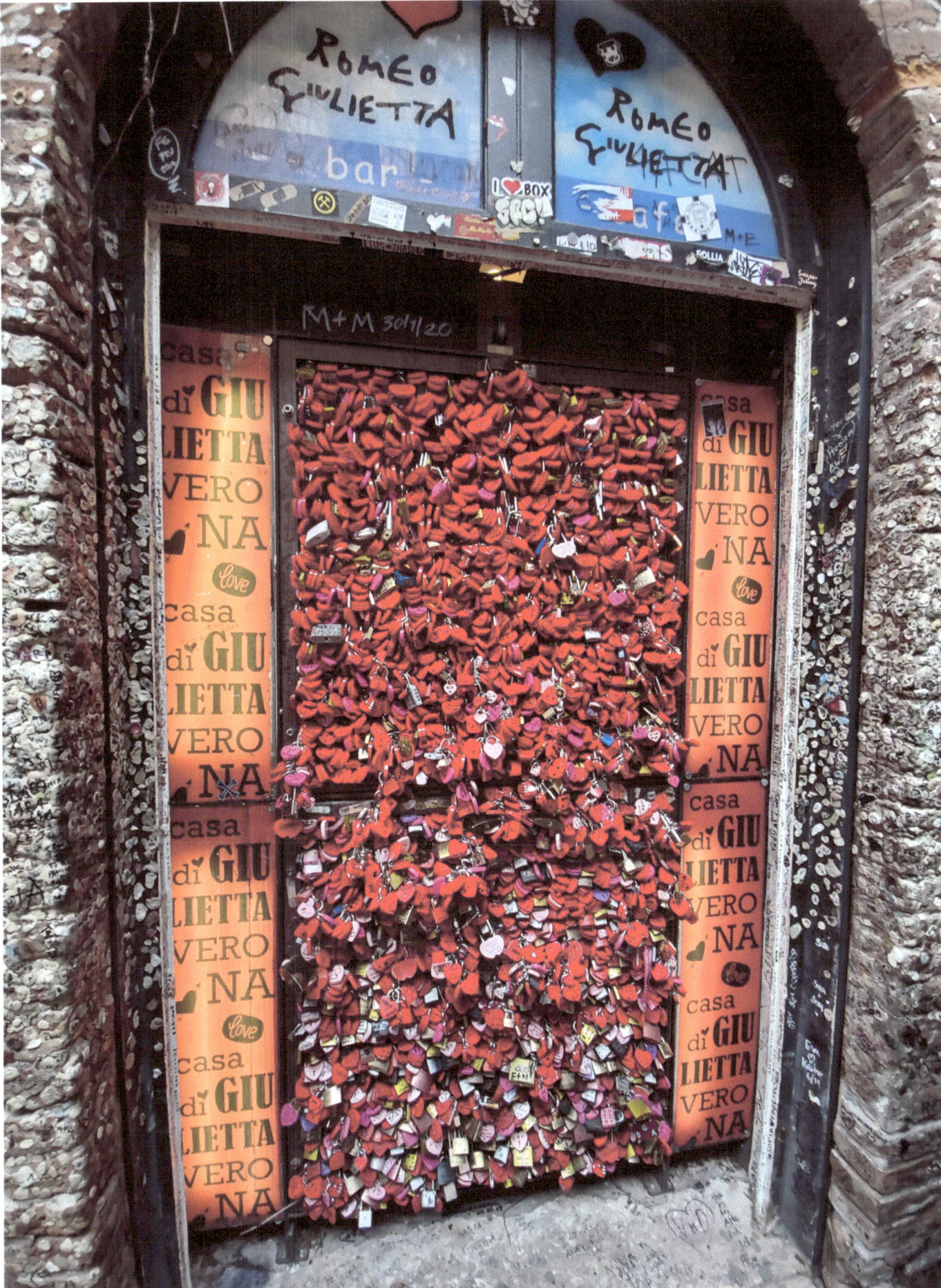

"Oh, I am fortune's fool!"
Romeo (act 3, scene 1)

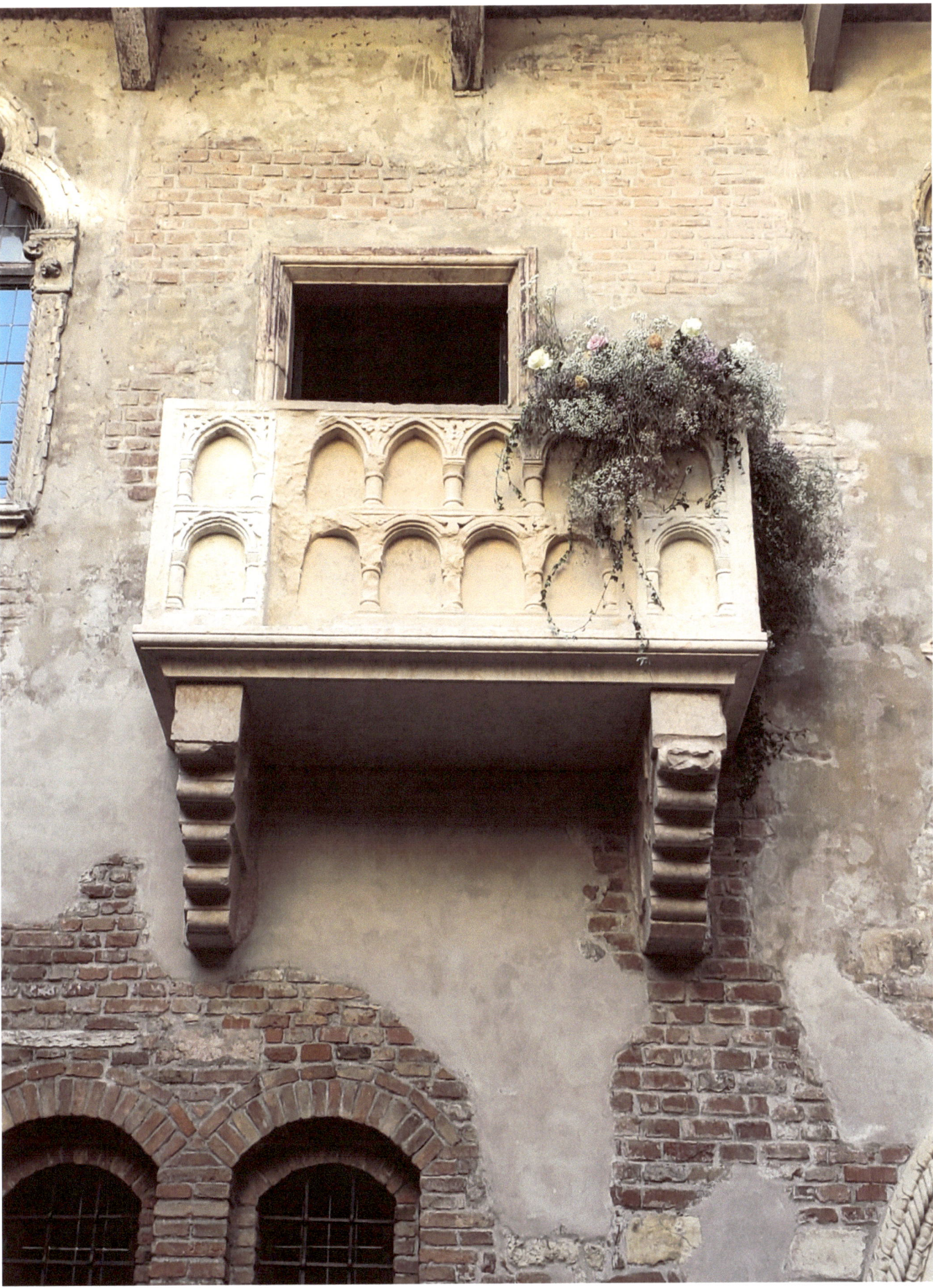

"Give me my Romeo, and, when I shall die,
Take him and cut him out in little stars,
And he will make the face of heaven so fine
That all the world will be in love with night,
And pay no worship to the garish sun."
Juliet (act 3, scene 2)

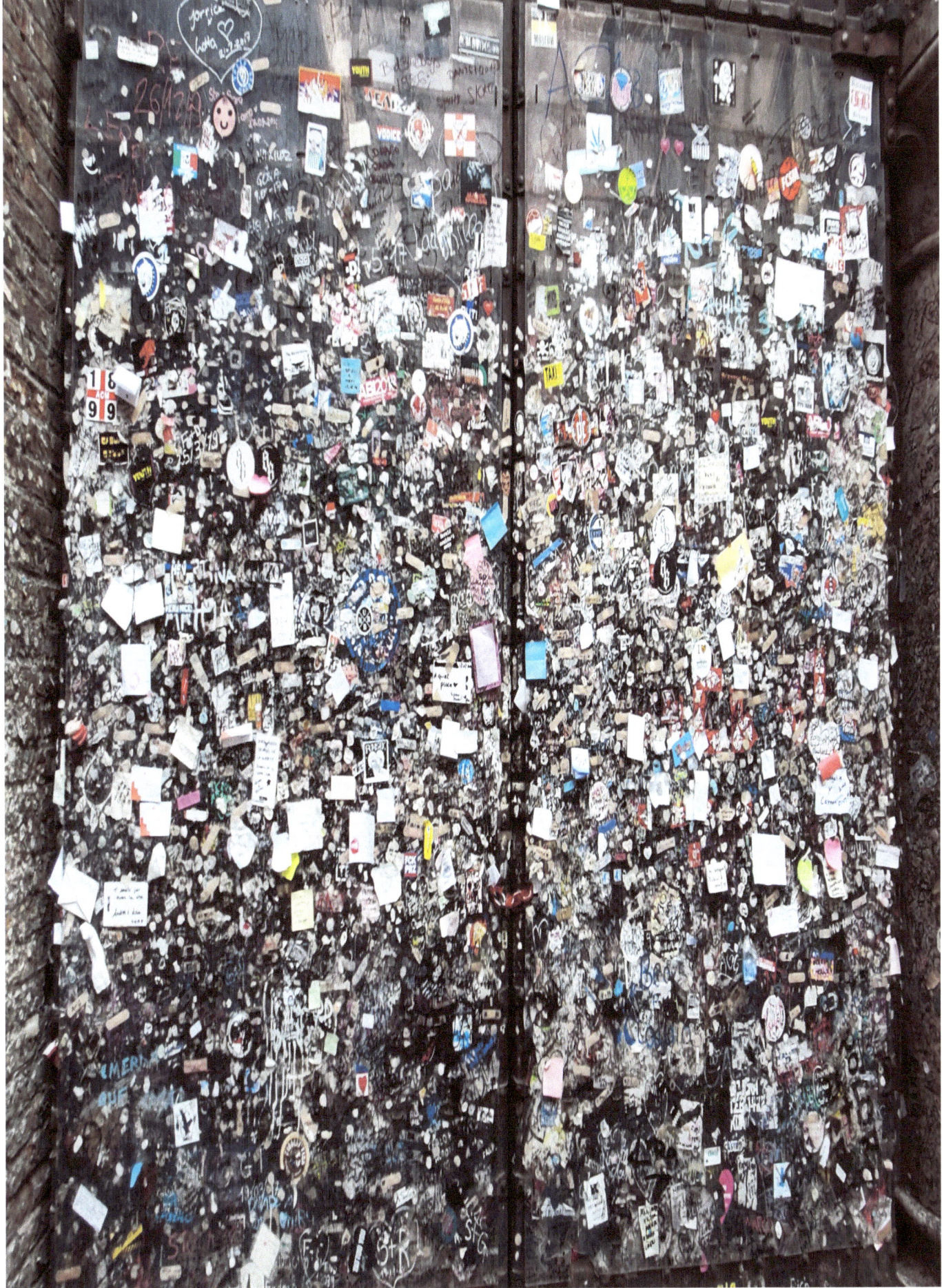

"Romeo, Romeo, Romeo! Here's drink: I drink to thee."

Juliet (Act 4, Scene 3)

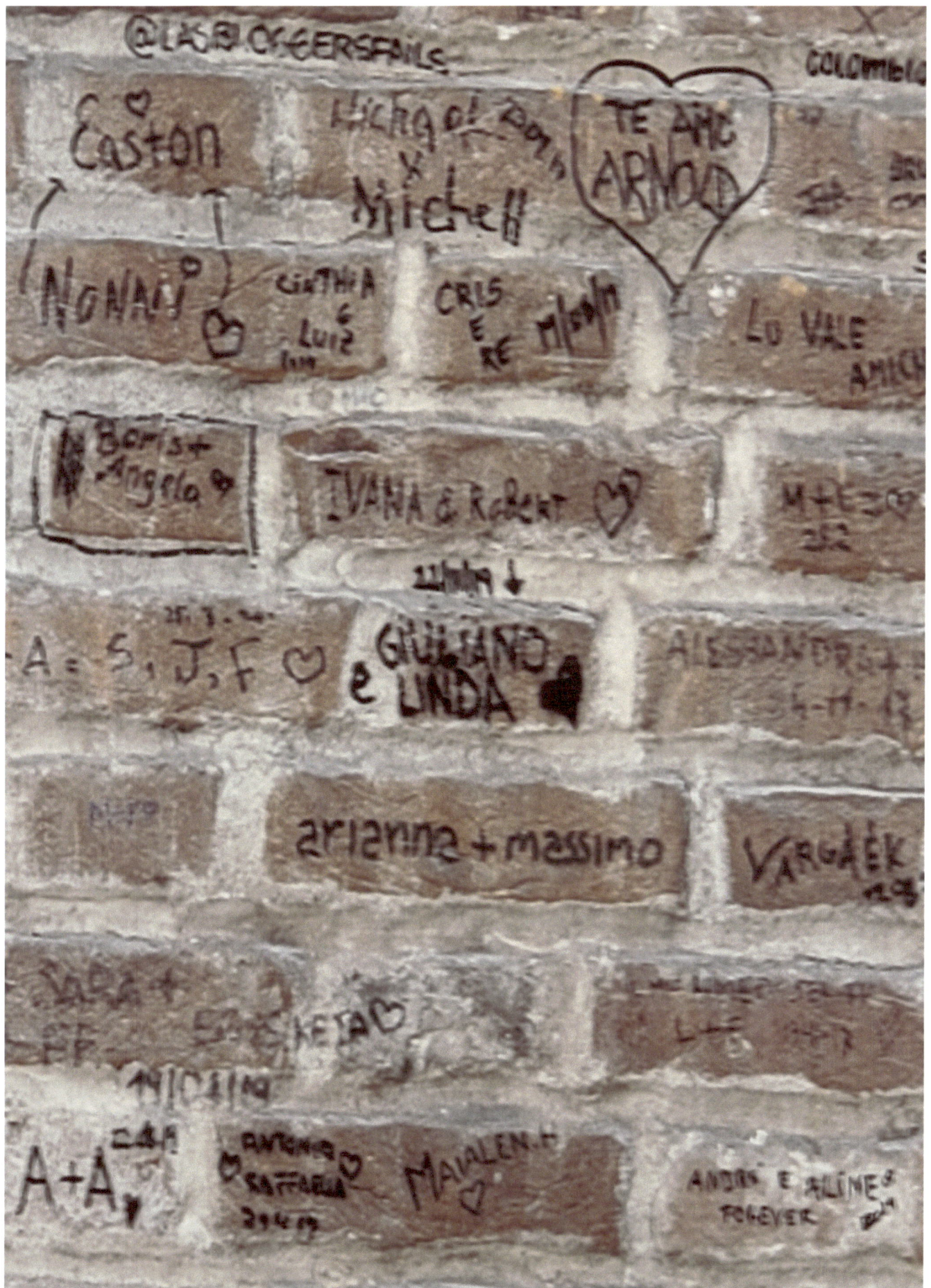

"O true apothecary, Thy drugs are quick. Thus with a kiss I die."
Romeo (act 5, scene 3)

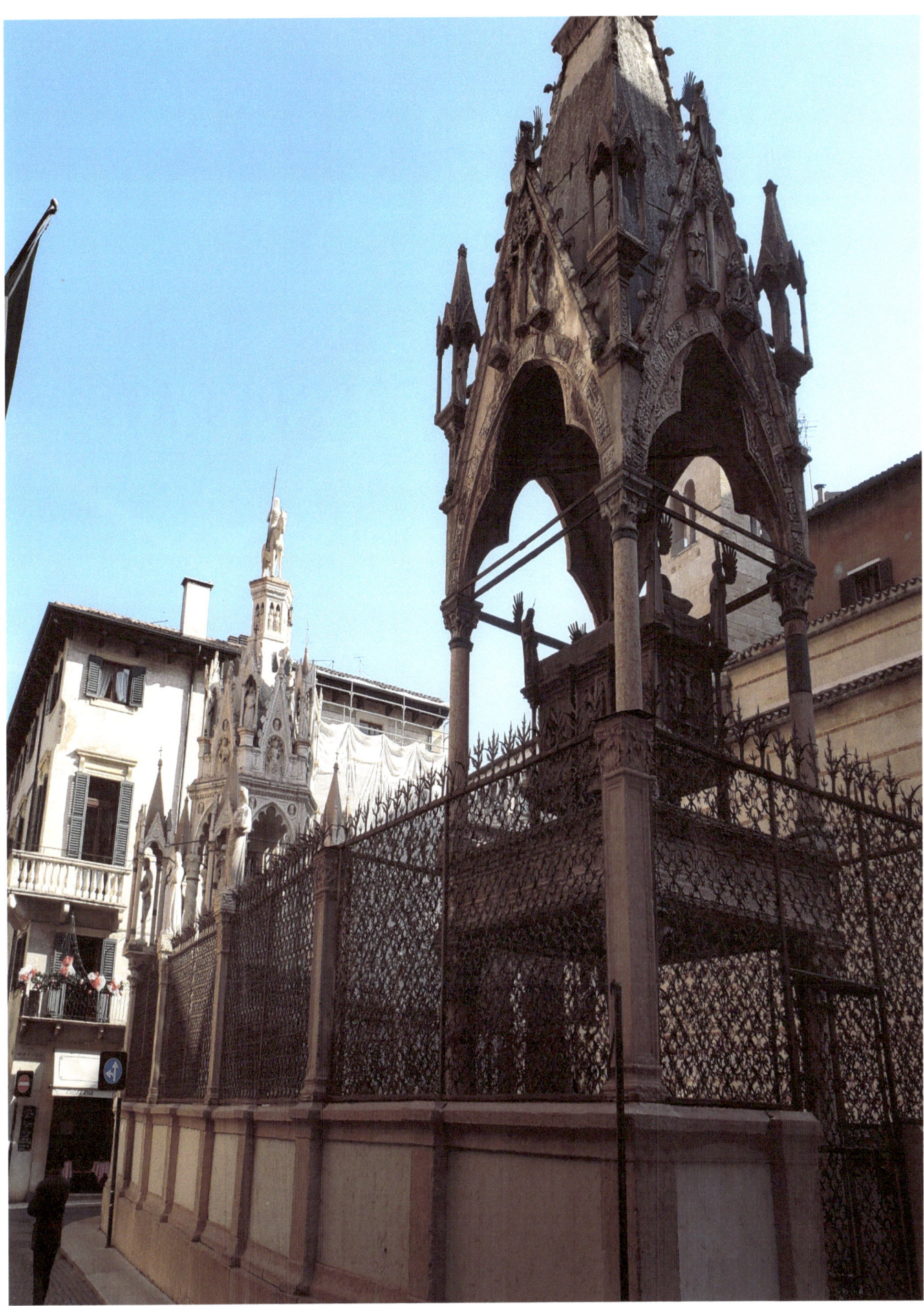

"Tempt not a desperate man"

Romeo (act 5, scene 3)

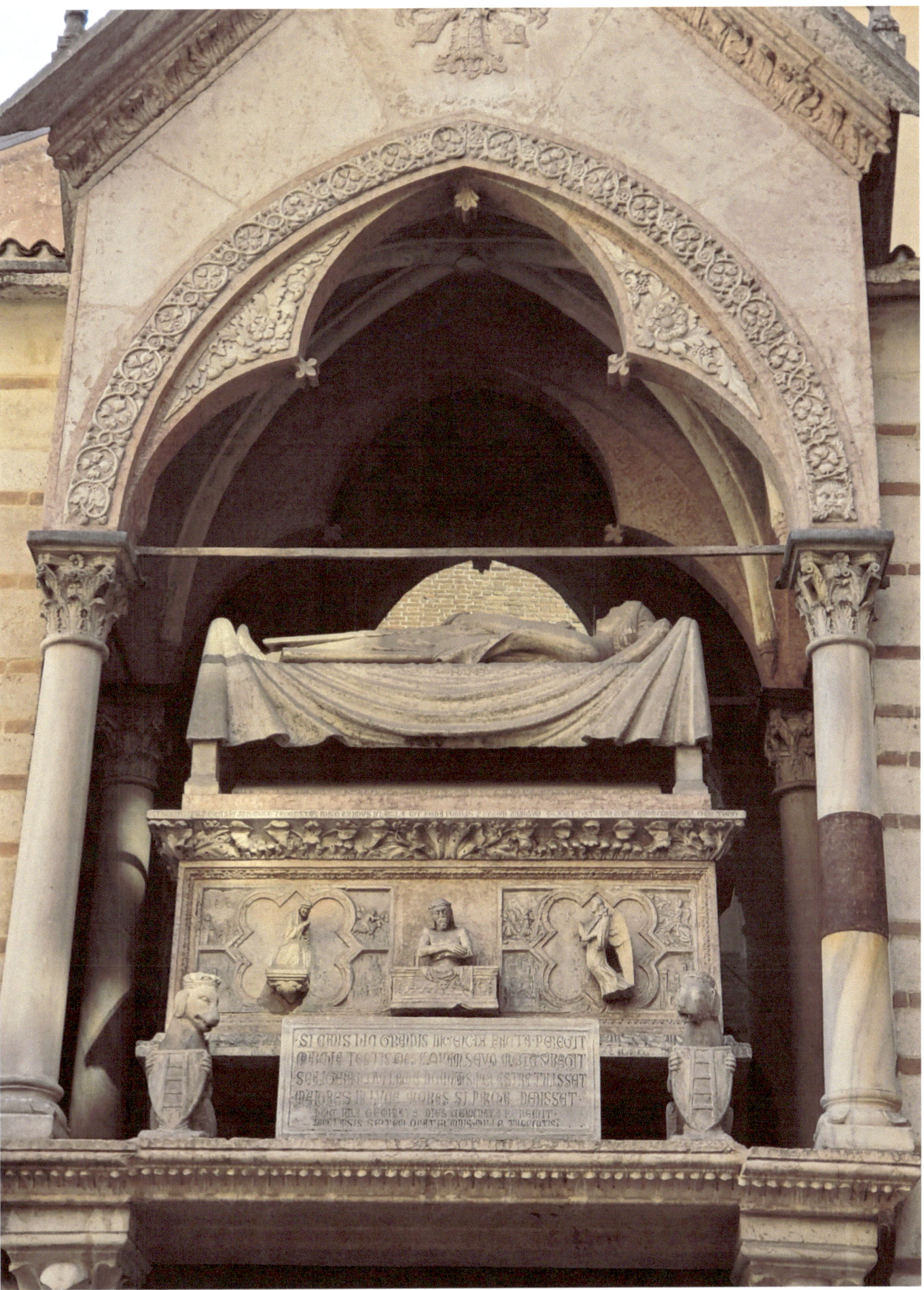

"O happy dagger, This is thy sheath: there rust, and let me die."
Juliet (act 5, scene 3)

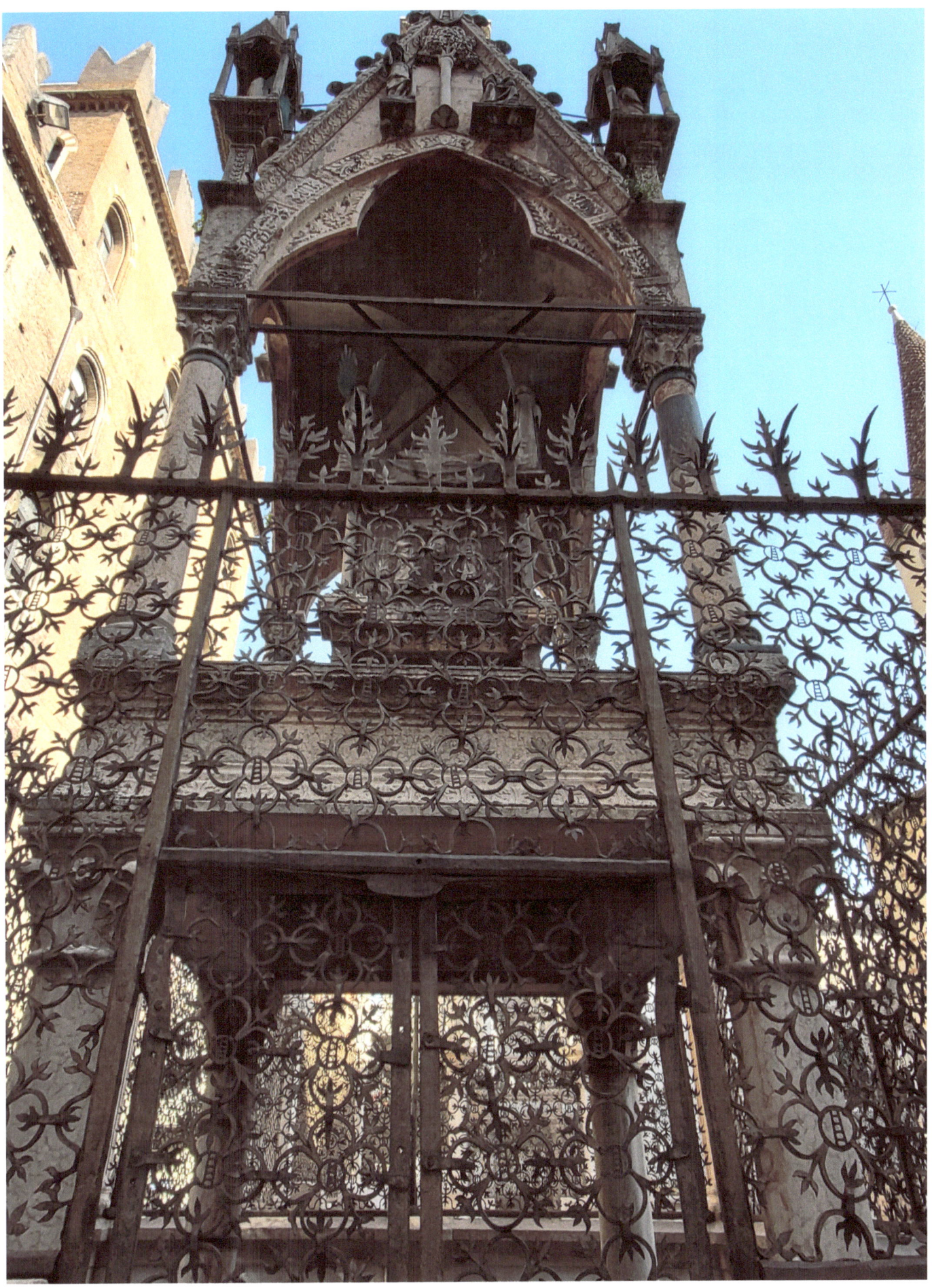

"All are punished."
Prince (act 5, scene 3)

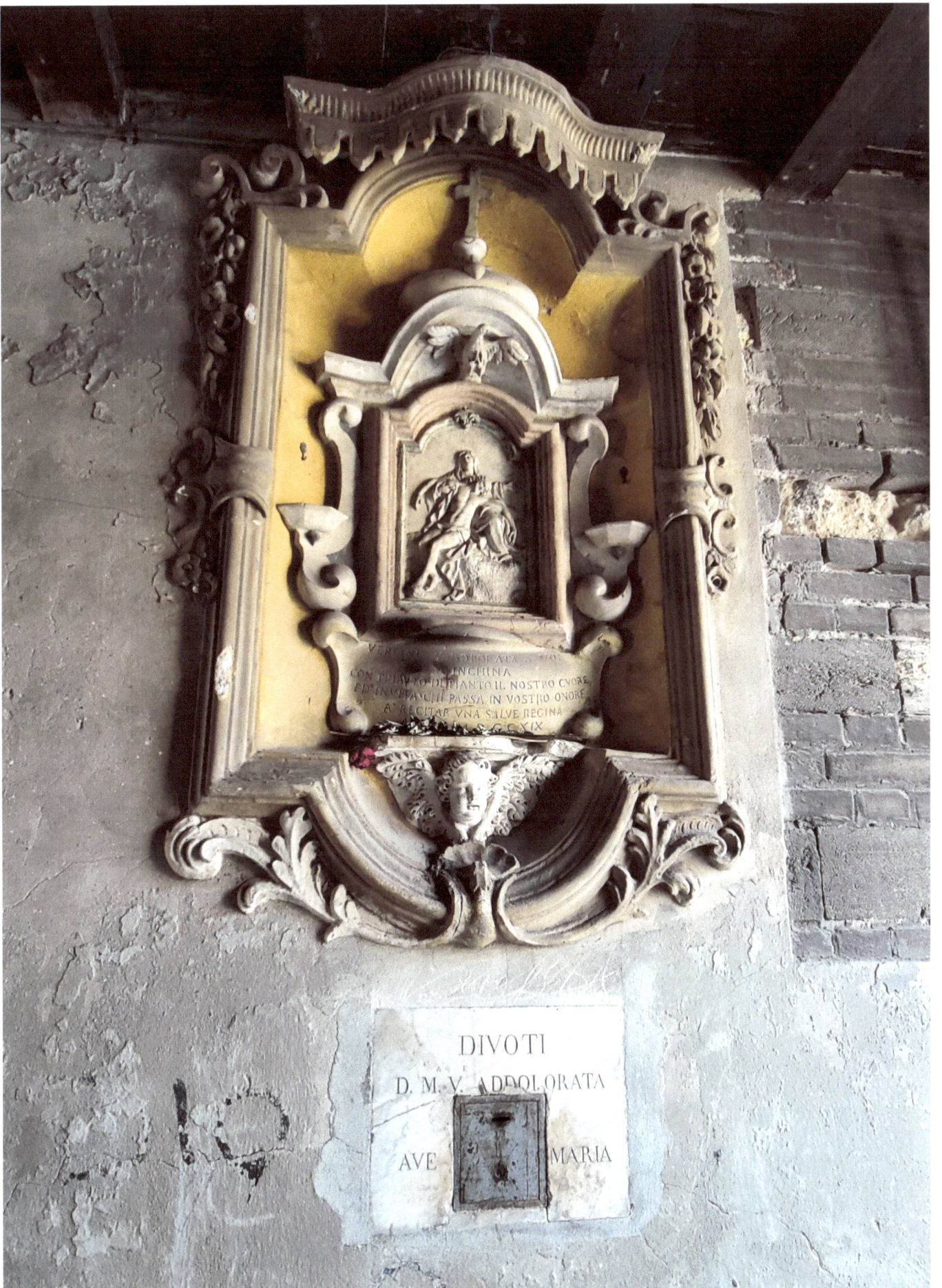

DIVOTI
D. M. V. ADDOLORATA

AVE    MARIA

"For never was a story of more woe

Than this of Juliet and her Romeo."

Prince (act 5, scene 3)

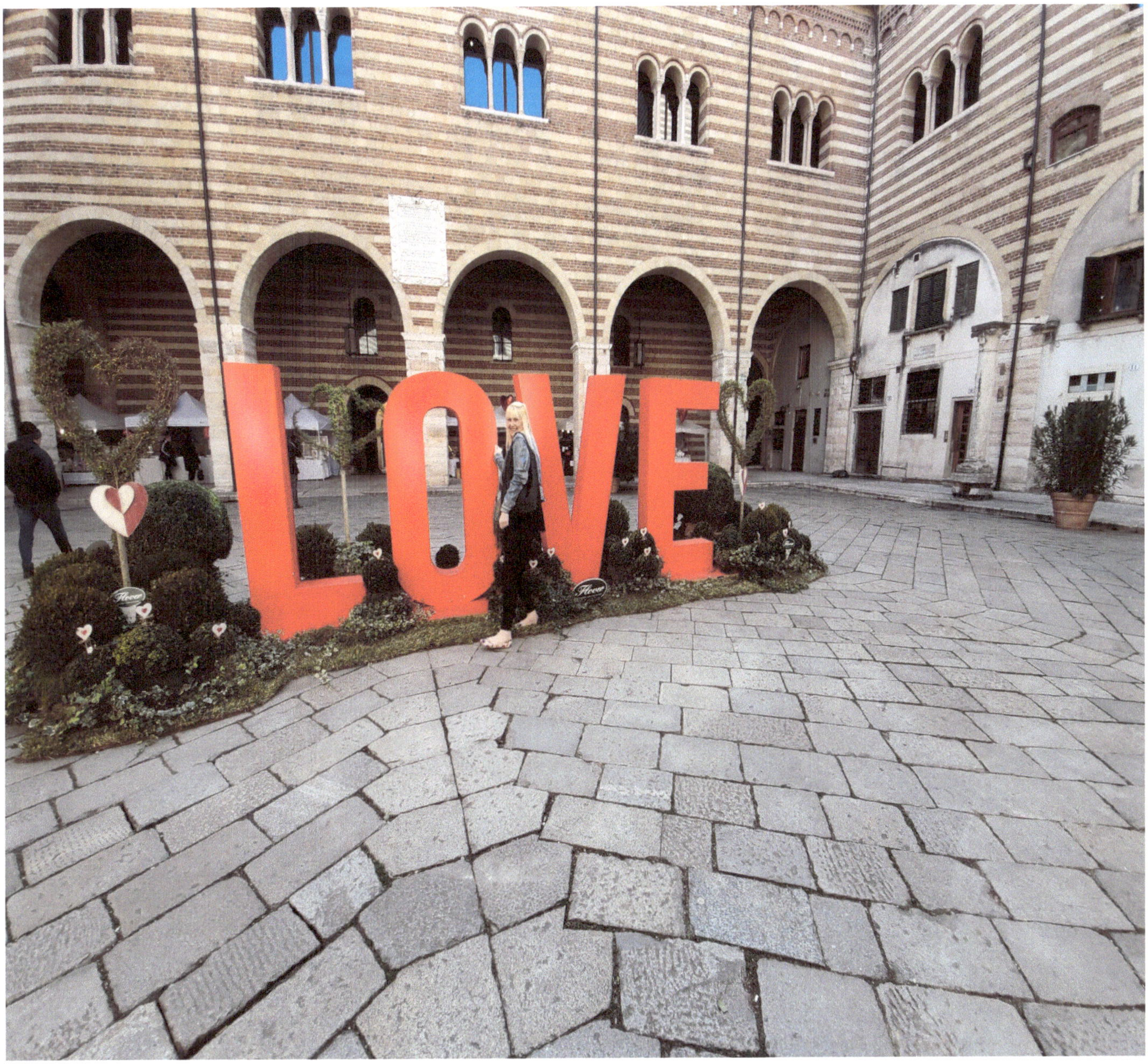

This book is dedicated to all the romantics out there ( me being one of them )

Live love laugh

*Linda Larson*

# Verona, Italy, Feb 2020

I hope you enjoyed my photos & recap of Romeo & Juliet

## More books to enjoy

Jewels of Italy 2020

British Columbia day dreaming

Valentine ideas for everyone

www.ingramcontent.com/pod-product-compliance
Lightning Source LLC
Chambersburg PA
CBHW051207220526
45473CB00003B/938